Copyright © 2024 by Scott Palmer

ISBN: 978-1-0882-1232-5 All rights reserved. No part of this book may be reproduced or transmitted in any form or by any means, electronic or mechanical, including photocopying, recording, or by any information storage and retrieval system, without permission from the copyright owner.

Published by Cypress Hills Press
Brooklyn, New York

Book design: Richard Tackett
https://www.facebook.com/TackettDesign

JACK THE RIPPER ON FILM & TV

BY

SCOTT PALMER

INTRODUCTION

This is a reference book dealing with selected motion picture and television productions having to do with the character known as Jack the Ripper, who terrorized the East End of London in the Autumn of 1888.

The book includes all productions in date order, with directorial credits, running times, complete cast listings, numerous photographs (including film posters), and a story synopsis for each entry.

Twenty productions are included, ranging from the 1926 silent Alfred Hitchcock film *The Lodger*, up to the 2001 production *From Hell*, starring Johnny Depp.

There are fourteen theatrically-released motion pictures, covering a period of 75 years, as well as six made for television productions, including a 1988 TV documentary.

Alfred Hitchcock directed the first Jack the Ripper film in 1926, based on the novel by Marie Belloc Lownes. Film star Ivor Novello had the script changed to reveal the Lodger as an innocent man.

When talking pictures came into being, Novello decided that he wanted to remake *The Lodger*, which was done in 1932. It copied the Hitchcock film and was extremely popular with audiences and critics.

In 1944, 20th Century Fox produced The *Lodger*, starring Laird Cregar as Mr. Slade (he took his name from a nearby street sign). Returning to the basis of the novel, Slade is revealed to be Jack the Ripper at the end of the film.

The Man in the Attic, made in 1953, starred Jack Palance in the title role. Slade rents an attic room from a middle-aged couple in London, and the film remains faithful to the original novel.

Other films followed, such as the 1959 film *Jack the Ripper*, in which Jack is shown to be a vengeful doctor who meets a grisly fate, and *A Study in Terror* (1965), which pits Sherlock Holmes against Jack the Ripper.

Hands of the Ripper (1971) saw the 2-year-old daughter of Jack the Ripper witnessing a murder; 15 years later, she is a troubled young girl who is seemingly possessed by the spirit of her late father. While in a psychotic trance she continues his murderous spree, but has no recollection of the events afterwards.

Klaus Kinski took on the title role in 1976, and 1979 saw two excellent films, *Murder By Decree*, starring Christopher Plummer as Sherlock Holmes, and *Time After Time*, with Malcolm McDowell as H.G. Wells and David Warner as Jack the Ripper. In 2001, Johnny Depp starred in *From Hell*, as police Inspector Frederick Abberline.

There have been a number of instances where the character was played on TV; I have listed six of the most prominent productions, including episodes of *The Veil, Thriller*, and *Kolchak: The Night Stalker,* as well as the 1973 production *Jack the Ripper*.

To mark the 100th Anniversary of the murders, a two-part film called *Jack the Ripper* was made for TV, starring Michael Caine as detective Abberline. As like *Murder By Decree*, attention was paid to sets, costumes, locations, and many fine actors graced the notable cast.

TABLE OF CONTENTS

1926-The Lodger..7

1932-The Lodger..15

1944-The Lodger..23

1950-Room to Let..33

1953-Man in the Attic..41

1958-The Veil: Jack the Ripper...51

1959-Jack the Ripper...59

1961-Thriller: Yours Truly, Jack the Ripper.....................69

1964-The Monster of London City....................................75

1965-A Study in Terror..81

1971-Hands of the Ripper..95

1973-Jack the Ripper..103

1974-Kolchak: The Night Stalker: The Ripper................127

1976-Jack the Ripper..133

1979-Murder By Decree...139

1979-Time After Time..151

1988-Jack the Ripper..159

1988-The Secret Identity of Jack the Ripper...................171

1997-The Ripper...177

2001-From Hell..183

THE LODGER (1926)

DIRECTED BY ALFRED HITCHCOCK

CAST

Ivor Novello	The Lodger
June	Daisy Bunting
Malcolm Keen	Joe
Marie Ault	Mrs. Bunting
Arthur Chesney	Mr. Bunting
Reginald Gardiner	Dancer
Eve Gray	Ripper Victim
Alfred Hitchcock	Man in Newspaper Office
Alma Reville	Woman Listening to Wireless

Ivor Novello

June

Malcolm Keen

Marie Ault

Arthur Chesney

Reginald Gardiner

Alfred Hitchcock

Alma Reville

Doctor

68 minutes

Jack the Ripper (referred to here as "The Avenger') murders yet another woman. All the victims are blonde. At a fashion show that night, model Daisy Bunting and other girls are nervous.

Back at Daisy's home, her parents have been reading about the killings. Later that evening, a young man arrives to inquire about a room for rent. After seeing the room, the man decides to take it, and pays Mrs. Bunting a month's rent in advance.

The Lodger handcuffed on a fence

Arthur Chesney, Marie Ault

The Lodger, all muffled up

Book Cover   Film Poster

Arthur Chesney, Marie Ault

The man turns all the portraits of women-which hang on the wall-facing backwards so as not to look at them; when Daisy arrives to remove them, there is an immediate attraction between her and the lodger.

This causes an ill feeling from Joe, Daisy's boyfriend-who happens to be a policeman investigating the murders. One night, Mrs. Bunting hears the lodger go out. She goes into his room and tries to open a cupboard, which is locked. Early in the morning, another woman is found murdered in the next street.

Mrs. Bunting greets the Lodger

Marie Ault in her bed

Malcolm Keen as Joe

Mrs. Bunting tells her husband she is convinced the lodger is The Avenger, and tries to prevent him from being alone with Daisy. When Daisy sneaks out late one night with the lodger, Joe follows them. Daisy is angered and says she doesn't want to see Joe any more. Joe now thinks the lodger is The Avenger..

Ivor Novello as The Lodger

French Film Poster

Ivor Novello, June, Malcolm Keen

Armed with a warrant, Joe returns to the Bunting home and searches the lodger's room. Accompanied by two other policeman, the trio discovers a number of suspicious things, including a gun in a small black bag, along with newspaper clippings about the murders, and a map of the murder sites.

A terrifying scream!

June and Ivor Novello

Malcolm Keen, Arthur Chesney

Most damning is a photograph of the first victim. The lodger is subsequently arrested, but manages to escape. Daisy finds him, handcuffed and shivering, and takes him to a pub. He tells her that the first victim was his sister, and he swore to find the Avenger and bring him to justice.

The Lodger comes to rent a room

Marie Ault, Arthur Chesney

Ivor Novello, Marie Ault

Meanwhile, a suspicious group of locals put upon the lodger, cornering him and beating him. Joe tries to intervene, telling them that the real Avenger has been caught, but they only stop the beating when a newsboy announces the Avenger has been caught. Some time later, the lodger recovers from his injuries, and heads off with Daisy.

Ivor Novello & June

Arthur Chesney and Marie Ault

Marie Ault looks surprised

June, Malcolm Keen, Marie Ault

THE LODGER (1932)

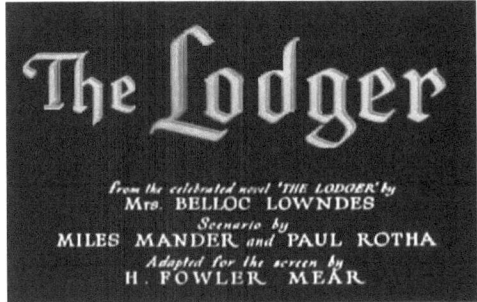

DIRECTED BY MAURICE ELVEY

CAST

Ivor Novello..................Michael Angeloff
Elizabeth Allan...................Daisy Bunting
A.W. Baskcomb...............George Bunting
Barbara Everest....................Mrs. Bunting
Jack Hawkins............................Joe Martin
Peter Gawthorne...............Lord Southcliff
Kynaston Reeves...................Bob Mitchell
Shayle Gardner..................Detective Snell
Drusilla Wills...........................Mrs. Coles
Antony Holles................................Silvano
George Merritt....................Commissioner
Mollie Fisher.........................Gladys Sims
Andrea Malandrinos........Mr. Rabinovitch
Harold Meade...............................Coroner
Ian Wilson.....................Newspaper Seller
Iris Ashley...Police Commissioner's Daughter

Ivor Novello  Elizabeth Allan A.W. Baskcomb

Barbara Everest Jack Hawkins Peter Gawthorne

Kynaston Reeves Shayle Gardner Drusilla Wills

Antony Holles George Merritt Mollie Fisher

Andrea Malandrinos Harold Meade Ian Wilson Iris Ashley Actress Man 1 Man 2

Man 3   Man 4   Woman 1   Woman 2   Woman 3

67 minutes

London newspapers proclaim another "telephone box" murder by a killer known as The Avenger. After discussing the news, George Bunting and his wife Evelyn debate their own circumstances, and the impossibility of paying their bills unless they quickly secure a new lodger.

Ivor Novello, Elizabeth Allan

A.W. Baskcomb, Barbara Everest

Jack Hawkins, Ivor Novello

Working at the local telephone exchange, the Buntings' daughter, Daisy overhears something peculiar: a call cut off by a cry. She reports it to her supervisor.

Lord Southcliff, the owner of the Evening Sun newspaper, tells his reporters that a Bosnian criminologist called Silvano is travelling to London to investigate the possibility of the Avenger being a man who escaped an asylum in Zagreb some time previously.

Peter Gawthorne has a cigar

Peter Gawthorne, Kynaston Reeves

Detectives arrest the Lodger

17

Lord Southcliff singles out ambitious young reporter Joe Martin and instructs him to focus on the Avenger case to the exclusion of all else.

At the Buntings,' a knock on the door heralds the arrival of a man in search of rooms to let, who introduces himself as Michel Angeloff. Mrs. Bunting is grateful over this turn in her family's luck, and sends Daisy upstairs with a cup of tea.

Book Cover   U.S. Film Poster

Elizabeth Allan, Ivor Novello, Barbara Everest

Jack Hawkins, Andrea Malandrinos

Ivor Novello, Elizabeth Allan

Elizabeth Allan, Jack Hawkins

Already intrigued by the dark stranger, Daisy does so with alacrity, listening admiringly as the lodger plays upon the piano in his room. The two fall into conversation, and Daisy is startled and amused when Angeloff proclaims the telephone "a horrible invention."

Meanwhile, Joe Martin arrives, and Mr. Bunting criticizes him for his failure to collect Daisy after work, as promised. Joe shrugs this off, insisting that his job had to come first. Daisy, too, is cold to Joe. He tries to win her over by revealing details of the Avenger's most recent murder, but when he tells how the victim had her throat cut in a public telephone box, Daisy becomes ill, suddenly certain that she actually heard the murder.

Joe immediately telephones his editor, Bob Mitchell, and gives him the story, including Daisy's name and address. He also snatches a photograph of Daisy before running off. The next day, Daisy' picture and story are in all the newspapers.

Police holding a briefing

Poster about the Avenger

A.W. Baskcomb, Jack Hawkins, Barbara Everest

Angeloff reads the account of the latest killing, and discusses it with Mrs. Bunting. When she proclaims the killer "a beast" he speaks heatedly, arguing that perhaps the killer cannot help himself. When Mrs. Bunting says that the killer should be put out of his misery, Angeloff agrees.

He then asks her to remove from his room the pictures of women that decorate his walls, explaining nervously that he is used to bare walls. Daisy gives evidence at the inquest on the latest victim. Her father also attends, as does Angeloff.

And Mr. Silvano, the Bosnian expert who testifies that the London killer is Stefan Obolovitch, an escapee from the Zagreb State Asylum. Silvano goes on to describe Obolovitch's background: his respectable family, his musical training, and the disastrous marriage that apparently triggered his mania against women.

U.S. Film Poster

Ivor Novello with violin

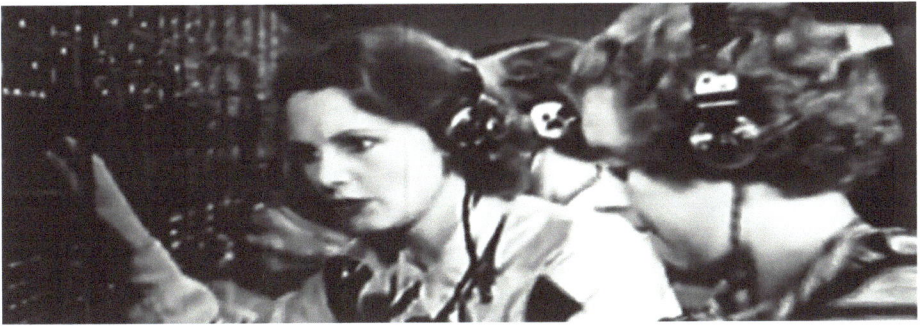

Elizabeth Allan on the switchboard

As he speaks, Angeloff slips unobtrusively from the room. Later the police arrive at the Bunting home having decided that Angeloff is really Stefan Obolovitch. They handcuff him but he manages to escape out into the foggy night.

Daisy meanwhile is at the park to meet him, and hails a figure in the fog who looks like Angeloff. When Angeloff arrives, the Avenger is finally identified and dealt with, and all is explained.

Peter Gawthorne, Jack Hawkins, Kynaston Reeves

Jack Hawkins, Elizabeth Allan, Ivor Novello

THE LODGER (1944)

DIRECTED BY JOHN BRAHM

CAST

Laird Cregar	Slade
Merle Oberon	Kitty Langley
George Sanders	Inspector John Warwick
Sir Cedric Hardwicke	Robert Bonting
Sara Allgood	Ellen Bonting
Queenie Leonard	Daisy
Aubrey Mather	Supt. Sutherland
Doris Lloyd	Jennie
Frederick Worlock	Sir Edward Willoughby
David Clyde	Sergeant Bates
Helena Pickard	Annie Rowley
Harry Allen	Conductor
Jimmy Aubrey	Cab Driver
Wilson Benge	Vigilante
Billy Bevan	Bartender
Ted Billings	News Vendor
Edmond Breon	Manager
Mae Bruce	Screaming Woman
Olaf Hytten	Harris
Colin Campbell	Harris Assistant
Ruth Clifford	Hairdresser
Herbert Clifton	Conductor
Grace Davies	Chorus Girl
Harold De Becker	Charlie
Cyril Delevanti	Stagehand
Frank Elliott	Aide
Herbert Evans	Constable

Laird Cregar  — Merle Oberon — George Sanders

Sir Cedric Hardwicke — Sara Allgood — Queenie Leonard

Aubrey Mather — Doris Lloyd — Frederick Worlock

David Clyde — Helena Pickard — Harry Allen

Jimmy Aubrey — Wilson Benge — Billy Bevan

Douglas Gerrard..............................Porter
Kit Guard................................Pub Patron
Charlie Hall.............................Comedian
Gerald Hamer............................Milkman
Lumsden Hare......................Dr. Sheridan
Alec Harford............................Conductor
Forrester Harvey..........................Cobbler
Stuart Holmes...................Prince Edward
Kenneth Hunter..........Mounted Inspector
Crauford Kent........................King's Aide
Skelton Knaggs.................Man With Cart
Charles Knight...........................Vigilante
John Rogers....................Down and Outer
Raymond Severn...............................Boy
Anita Sharp-Bolster........................Wiggy
C. Montague Shaw............Stage Manager
Will Stanton...............................Newsboy
Donald Stuart................Concertina Player
Walter Tetley..............................Call Boy
David Thursby............................Sergeant
Heather Wilde......................Mary Bowles
Colin Hunter, Boyd Irwin, John Rice,
Yorke Sherwood.......................Policemen
Colin Kenny, Charles Morgan, Leslie
Sketchley, Robert Stephenson...................
....Plainclothesmen

AND: Joan Bayley, Barbara Burns, Jean Carroll, Laverne Dell, Dorothy Dinwiddie, Fern Gey, Iris Gordon, Barbara Hallstone, Margaret Lee, Connie Leon, Lolita Lindsay, Jean Lucisuis, Shyrle Martinson, Carmen Moreno, Edmund Mortimer, Dolly Perrin, Ethel Sherman, Louise Snyder, Jane Starr, Jean Sturgeon, Daphne Vane, Beverly Weaver

Ted Billings

Edmond Breon

Mae Bruce

Olaf Hytten

Colin Campbell

Ruth Clifford

Herbert Clifton

Harold De Becker

Cyril Delevanti

Frank Elliott

Herbert Evans

Douglas Gerrard

Kit Guard

Charlie Hall

Gerald Hamer

Lumsden Hare

Alec Harford

Forrester Harvey

Stuart Holmes

Kenneth Hunter

Crauford Kent

84 minutes

In 1888, after the man known as Jack the Ripper has committed three murders, late Victorian London is terrified. In Whitechapel, with so many police around, a woman named Katie feels safe going to her room; she turns through an archway, where a man kills her.

A large man with a mustache wearing an overcoat and carrying an oilcloth bag rents rooms from Mr. and Mrs. Bonting. He identifies himself as Mr. Slade. Robert Bonting doesn't like having a stranger in the house, but the man had paid an entire month's rent in advance.

Aubrey Mather, George Sanders

25

When Ellen brings supper, she finds Slade has turned the photographs of actresses decorating his room to the wall, complaining that their eyes followed him; Ellen's niece Kitty, a musical performer, also lives in the house.

Slade goes to Whitechapel, where Kitty is opening her new stage act. At the theatre, Annie Rowley, who had been a performer, meets Kitty, then leaves.

Laird Cregar, Merle Oberon

David Clyde, George Sanders

Laird Cregar as Slade

After the show, Inspector Warwick of Scotland Yard comes to the theatre and announces that Annie Rowley is the latest Ripper victim. He also says that all the murder victims were women who had once been on the stage.

Since someone saw the Ripper carrying a black oilcloth bag, Slade decides to burn the one he carries. Mr. Bonting remarks that it was a sensible thing to do-he also has a black bag, which he hid in a chest.

Doris Lloyd, Anita Sharp-Bolster    Lobby Card

The Lodger up in the gantry

27

Lobby Card   Lobby Card

Laird Cregar looking downstairs

Later Slade shows Kitty a miniature self-portrait painted by his late brother. Meanwhile Inspector Warwick takes an interest in the charming Kitty. With the police on the streets in force, the Ripper hides in a woman's room; when she returns, he kills her.

Back at the Bonting house, Kitty finds Slade burning his overcoat in the kitchen stove, claiming it was contaminated in an experiment. The next day Slade finds himself alone in the house with Kitty; he tells her it was the beauty of women that led his brother to destruction.

When Ellen meets Robert outside, they realize that Kitty must be alone with Slade, as Daisy the maid has gone out shopping. Robert hurries home.

As the police have fingerprints the Ripper left at a crime scene, Robert and Ellen tell him of their suspicions of Slade, and Warwick comes to the house to make a fingerprint comparison. When Warwick compares the Ripper's fingerprints with some on a glass Slade used, he finds they don't match, which clears him- unless the Ripper is left-handed.

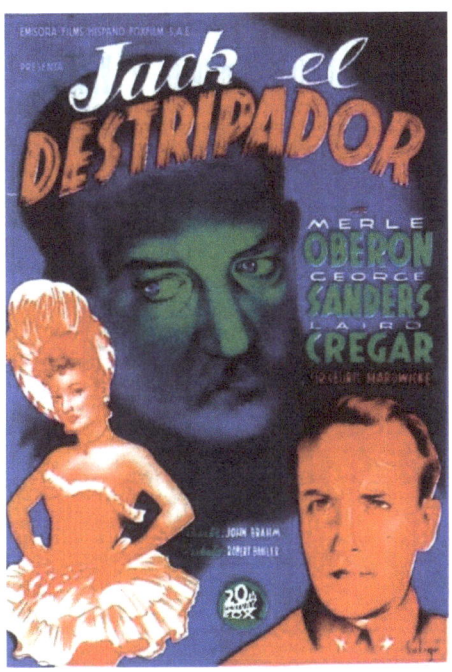

Foreign Film Poster

Sir Cedric Hardwicke, Laird Cregar

Laird Cregar, Queenie Leonard

After finding the portrait of Slade's brother, Warwick brings it to the theatre, and tells his superior, Superintendent Sutherland that Slade's brother was ruined by drink and a girl who was the first victim of Jack the Ripper.

After Kitty's performance, she goes to her dressing room to change and watch the rest of the show. However she soon discovers that there is someone else in the room-Slade. Slade locks the door, telling Kitty that she is exquisite, and that beauty should be reserved for him alone.

Helena Pickard, Merle Oberon

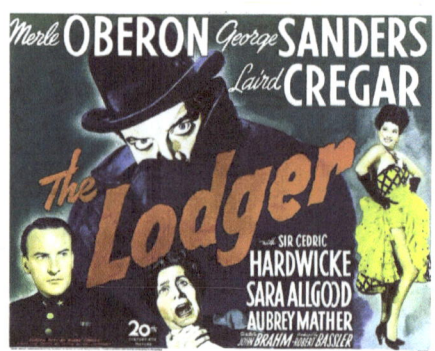

Film Poster

Slade takes his name from the street

When Kitty balks, he starts to strangle her, but she screams. Warwick breaks down the door and shoots Slade, wounding him as he escapes.

As the audience exits, Slade climbs to the stage flies, from which he tries to drop sandbags on Kitty.

Lobby Card

Sir Cedric Hardwicke, George Sanders

Laird Cregar as Mr. Slade

31

Police close in on the Ripper

Lobby Card

Laird Cregar, Merle Oberon

Sir Cedric Hardwicke, Queenie Leonard

Merle Oberon, Laird Cregar

Harold De Becker, Queenie Leonard

But thanks to Daisy's timely warning scream, he misses, and Warwick shoots him again. Knife in hand, cornered by the police, Slade throws himself through a closed window and into the Thames. He disappears.

32

ROOM TO LET (1950)

DIRECTED BY GODFREY GRAYSON

CAST

Valentine Dyall..............................Dr. Fell
Jimmy Hanley........................Curly Minter
Constance Smith.............Molly Musgrave
Christine Silver..................Mrs. Musgrave
Merle Tottenham...............................Alice
Charles Hawtrey................Mike Atkinson
Aubrey Dexter.............................Harding
J.A. La Penna..J.J.
Reginald Dyson.......Sergeant Cranbourne
Laurence Naismith...........................Editor
John Clifford...............................Atkinson
Stuart Saunders..............................Porter
Cyril Conway.........................Dr. Mansfield
Charles Houston.................................Tom
Harriet Petworth............................Matron
Charles Mander........................P.C. Smith
H. Hamilton Earle..........................Orderly
Frederick Kelsey.............................Butler
Archie Callum.................Nightwatchman

Valentine Dyall

Jimmy Hanley

Jimmy Hanley

Constance Smith

Christine Silver

Merle Tottenham

Charles Hawtrey Aubrey Dexter J.A. La Penna

Reginald Dyson Laurence Naismith John Clifford

Stuart Saunders

Cyril Conway

Charles Houston

Harriet Petworth

Charles Mander

H. Hamilton Earle Frederick Kelsey

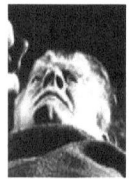

Archie Callum

68 minutes

Over drinks with two friends, an elderly Curly Minter recounts his experiences as a young journalist. The aging former journalist tells the story of his last investigative piece written in 1904.

Cyril Conway, Jimmy Hanley

Valentine Dyall, Christine Silver

Curly climbs up the ladder

Sergeant and Curly run to the house

Constance Smith, Jimmy Hanley

Reginald Dyson, Jimmy Hanley,
Cyril Conway

Jimmy Hanley, Charles Hawtrey,
Constance Smith

Valentine Dyall as Dr. Fell

Following a fire at a psychiatric hospital, a dying nightwatchman tells Minter that the fire was started deliberately by a patient who then escaped. However for some reason everyone seems to deny this.

35

When the asylum director claims that all of his patients are accounted for, Minter's story is pulled by his editor. Minter refuses to let it go and starts digging deeper.

Elsewhere, in London's East End, Dr. Fell arrives at a lodging house run by the wheelchair-bound Mrs. Musgrave and her daughter Molly who have a room to let.

Charles Hawtrey, Jimmy Hanley, Constance Smith

Constance Smith, Christine Silver, Jimmy Hanley, Valentine Dyall

Merle Tottenham, Christine Silver

Stuart Saunders, Jimmy Hanley, Constance Smith, Charles Hawtrey, John Clifford

Valentine Dyall, Merle Tottenham, Christine Silver, Constance Smith

Already sinister to begin with, Fell becomes decidedly abusive as he starts to manipulate the lives of the mother and daughter and their maid Alice, terrifying them into doing as he bids. For some reason he is allowed to take over the house. He talks in a menacing monotone. The lights are kept dim, the curtains drawn, his room locked and preventing other people from visiting.

Minter, a friend of Molly's, becomes involved and first suspects that Dr. Fell is in fact the escaped psychiatric patient and then to believe that he might actually be Jack the Ripper.

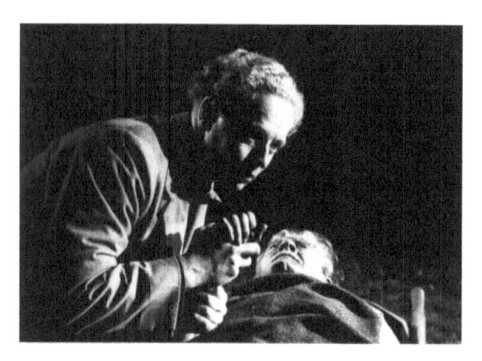

Jimmy Hanley, Archie Callum

Valentine Dyall, Christine Silver

Valentine Dyall sneaking around

Jimmy Hanley, Reginald Dyson

J.A. La Penna, Aubrey Dexter, Jimmy Hanley

Psychiatric hospital burns down

Continuing his investigation into the missing patient, Curly questions Sergeant Cranbourne. Curly and the Sergeant run to Mrs. Musgrave's house.

Having broken in to find Mrs. Musgrave lying at the foot of the stairs, the two head for the window of Dr. Fell's locked room. Followed by the Sergeant, Curly climbs up to where the two discover the Doctor's dead body. In the present, an elderly Curly walks home with his wife Molly after concluding his story.

Valentine Dyall, Constance Smith

Jimmy Hanley pours some tea

Constance Smith on the telephone

MAN IN THE ATTIC (1953)

DIRECTED BY HUGO FREGONESE

CAST

Jack Palance	Slade
Constance Smith	Lily Bonner
Byron Palmer	Inspector Warwick
Rhys Williams	William Harley
Frances Bavier	Helen Harley
Lester Matthews	Chief Insp. Melville
Harry Cording	Sergeant Bates
Ben Wright	Detective at Theatre
Sean McClory	Constable #1
Leslie Bradley	Constable #2
Tita Phillips	Daisy
Lisa Daniels	Mary Lenihan
Lillian Bond	Annie Rowley
Isabell Jewell	Katy
Arthur E. Gould-Porter	Man Making Toast
Ashley Cowan	Hospital Receptionist
Sylvia Lewis	Dancer
Mickey Martin	Messenger Boy
Rama Bai	Lelah
Joe Phillips	Constable
Bob Reeves	Coachman
Cosmo Sardo	Theatre Manager
Christopher Severn	Flower Delivery Boy
Arthur Tovey	Bar Patron
Chet Brandenburg, Michael Jeffers, Richard LaMarr	Townsmen

John Alban, Brandon Beach, Audrey Betz, Paul Bradley, Morgan Brown, George Calliga, Noble Chissell, James Conaty, Franklin Farnum, Joe Gilbert, Sam Harris, Stuart Holmes, Colin Kenny, Joseph La Cava, Carl Leviness, Monty O'Grady, Jeffrey Sayre, Scott Seaton, Norman Stevans..................................Theatre Patrons

Ashley Cowan Sylvia Lewis  Mickey Martin

Rama Bai  James Conaty  Franklin Farnum

Stuart Holmes  Colin Kenny  Jeffrey Sayre  Theatre Patron 1  Theatre Patron 2 Theatre Patron 3  Theatre Patron 4

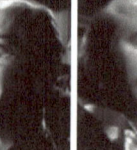

Theatre Patron 5

82 minutes

In 1888 the mysterious Jack the Ripper has just claimed his third victim. That very night, a man named Slade arrives at the home of William and Helen Harley looking to rent a room.

The Harleys have recently fallen upon financial difficulties, and despite William's displeasure with the idea, they are in no position to turn Slade away from their unused guest room.

German Film Poster

It's a nice living space, but the would-be lodger has something a little different in mind. Slade says that he is a pathologist by trade, and he requires a private space, isolated from the rest of the house, for those nights when he brings work home from the lab.

Fortunately for him, the Harleys have, in addition to the spare bedroom, a semi-finished attic, which proves to be exactly what he is looking for. Slade offers the Harleys five pounds a month, with the first two month's rent in advance, and Helen agrees to let him move in immediately.

Frances Bavier, Tita Phillips

Byron Palmer, Constance Smith, Lester Matthews

Slade's job keeps him on a schedule very different from most people's, and he frequently doesn't come home from the lab until well after midnight.

Thus it is scarcely surprising that Helen soon begins to suspect that her new lodger may be up to no good while he's out at all hours of the night, especially after the newspapers report that the police believe the Ripper may have some kind of medical or surgical training.

Foreign Film Poster

Frances Bavier, Byron Palmer

Rhys Williams, Frances Bavier

Jack Palance as Slade

William on the other hand doesn't give her worries any credence at all. Even after Helen finds the burned remains of Slade's black leather surgical bag in the spare bedroom's fireplace, William defends the lodger.

As a medical man himself, William has also found it expedient in the present climate of suspicion and paranoia to keep his surgeon's satchel out of sight. Indeed, William says that he'd have burned his, too, had he thought of it.

Meanwhile, the Harley household is about to become even more crowded. Their niece, Lily Bonner is returning from an extended visit to Paris.

Lily is a nightclub performer, and she has spent the months on the other side of the Channel recruiting a team of dancers fit to bring the more risque Parisian style of floor show to London. While Lily is in town, she's going to need a place to stay, and because the Harleys still have one more bedroom upstairs, they plan to take her in.

Film Poster

Lobby Card

Tweet! Looks like another murder

This soon brings Lily and Slade into contact, a meeting that is bound to be fraught with ramifications no matter what the reclusive boarder does with his nights out of the house. Lily takes an instant liking to Slade, and despite the man's professed aversion to actresses, he seems to return her interest. If Slade is just an odd but ultimately harmless shut-in, his budding relationship with Lily could potentially bring him out of his shell.

Constance Smith in the theatre

Death masks in the Black Museum

Then again, if Slade really is Jack the Ripper, Lily falls squarely into the target demographic for his victims. The clouds of suspicion swirling around Slade's head thickens on the night of Lily's first performance in London.

Before she goes on, she is visited in her dressing room by a woman named Annie Rowley, who had once been a regular attraction at the very club where Lily is dancing.

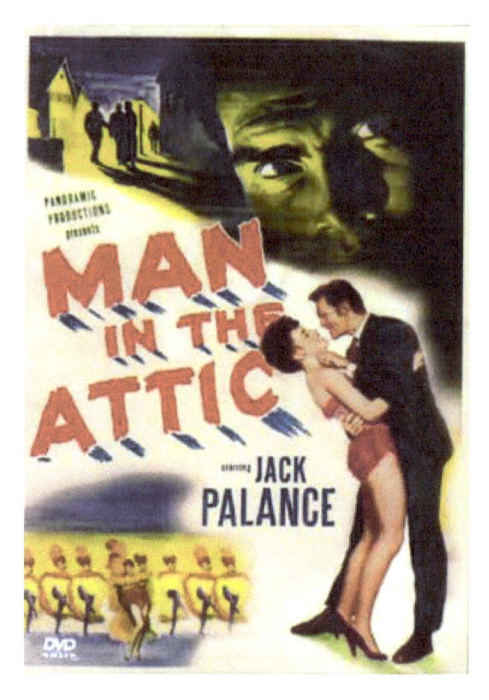

Film Poster

Constance Smith, Jack Palance

Jack Palance, Byron Palmer

Rhys Williams, Byron Palmer

Frances Bavier, Rhys Williams

Indeed, she was even assigned the same dressing room. Lily and Annie chat for a while, and then the ex-dancer leaves to return home. She never makes it, becoming Ripper victim number four in the alley behind the club.

Soon police Inspector Paul Warwick enters the case, and he comes to the Harley house the next day to conduct interviews. While he waits for Lily to return home, he learns about Slade's suspicious behavior from the Harleys' maid, Daisy.

As the investigation progresses, an unexpected factor comes into play, one which leads the detective to keep a rather closer eye on Slade than he might have otherwise. Warwick takes a liking to Lily, and that puts him into direct competition with the Harleys' lodger for the girl's affections. So is the noose of law that now begins slowly tightening around Slade's neck merely the product of Warwick's jealousy, or is the Man in the Attic really harboring a dark and deadly secret?

Tita Phillips, Rhys Williams

Rhys Williams, Byron Palmer

Harry Cording, Byron Palmer

THE VEIL-JACK THE RIPPER SEASON 1 EPISODE 11

Directed By David MacDonald Original Air Date: 1958

CAST

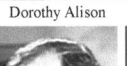

Boris Karloff...Host
Niall MacGinnis....................Walter Durst
Clifford Evans.........Inspector McWilliam
Dorothy Alison.......................Judith Durst
Nora Swinburne...............Mrs. Willowden
Charles Carson....................Dr. Hatherley
Robert Brown............................Constable
Mai Bacon...............................Fat Woman
Robert Brookes Turner...................Warder
Jeffrey Silk................................Policeman
John Timberlake.......................Conductor
Rita Tobin........................Coach Traveller
Delene Scott.............................Little Girl
Wallace Bosco, Bob E. Raymond............
................................Men in Police Station

This story concerns the dark and mysterious circumstances surrounding one of the most famous criminals in history: Jack the Ripper.

George Durst was a normal citizen of his time. A man completely average in all respects-all respects but one.

Niall MacGinnis, Clifford Evans

Niall MacGinnis as George Durst

One morning at breakfast, Durst tells his wife Judith that he had an odd and frightening dream. George knows that he has the ability to see into the future. In the dream, he was outside some horrible drinking house, and heard the ticking of a clock. The clock read 2:30. Then he saw a street sign that said Buck's Row.

His wife reads in the paper an account of the brutal murder of Mary Ann Nichols in Buck's Row, at 2:30 that morning. The crime was committed with a knife, and the suspect was said to have a considerable knowledge of surgery.

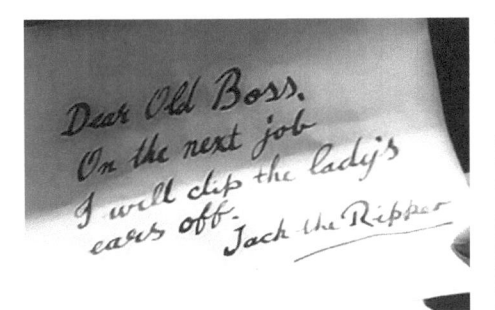

The Dear Boss Letter

Dorothy Alison, Niall MacGinnis

Niall MacGinnis as George Durst

53

Nora Swinburne, Clifford Evans, Charles Carson

Charles Carson, Clifford Evans, Niall MacGinnis

Judith tells George that it is his duty to go to the police, so he heads to the station. He is met by a constable who tells him that Inspector McWilliam is in charge of the case, but he will have to wait his turn as there are six other people waiting to see the Inspector. Durst leaves.

Next, one day Durst is walking down a street, and has a vision of another murder. This time he is wide awake, and it's broad daylight. He sees the dead woman wearing a red flower on her dress and was carrying a bunch of grapes. He and Mrs. Durst go again to Scotland Yard.

On the way, they are riding in a coach, when Durst gets an odd feeling and tells his wife "Jack the Ripper is on this bus." At Scotland Yard, Durst is able to see Inspector McWilliam.

Dorothy Alison & Niall MacGinnis

Durst tells him that a woman will soon be killed, and her ears will be severed from her head. Since the police received a note, allegedly from the killer, telling them that he will cut the next victim's ears off, McWilliam has Durst write a note to compare the handwriting.

McWilliam is now convinced that Durst knows way too much; he may in fact be the killer. So McWilliam has him thrown into a cell. While Durst is incarcerated, another two murders occur.

Boris Karloff as our host

In one of them, the victim's ears were clipped off, just as Durst had foreseen. Since Durst was behind bars when the murders happened, he is now in the clear and McWilliam is beginning to think that he is a genuine clairvoyant. He tells Durst the entire police force will be at his disposal.

Later, Durst gets the idea to use his gifts to locate the Ripper before he can kill again. Along with McWilliam and the constable, Durst walks the London streets, which eventually leads the trio to a fashionable house. "This is where the Ripper lives," Durst says.

Bucks Row Street sign

Dorothy Alison, Niall MacGinnis

The house is owned by a prominent surgeon named Willowden. Upon entering, they meet Mrs. Willowden and Dr. Hatherley. When they say they are there to see Dr. Willowden, they are told that he is dead. A coffin is on display in the drawing room. Durst wants to look inside the coffin, but Hatherley says that is outrageous. McWilliam says that he suspects Willowden knew something about the Whitechapel murders. Mrs. Willowden finally breaks down; she can't take it any more. Durst opens the coffin, which is filled with books.

Wallace Bosco, Woman, Bob E. Raymond

Delene Scott, Mai Bacon, Robert Brown

It seems that Willowden went insane. After sticking a hatpin through the paw of the family dog, he collected live bats, which he dipped in paraffin, and then set them on fire, cackling maniacally as they burned to death. Hatherley had him committed to an insane asylum near Edinburgh.

To spare the family's good name and to keep the scandal from the public, Hatherley signed a death certificate, stating that Dr. Willowden had died of a cerebral hemorrhage. Dr. Willowden now was beyond the reach of English law. But the slaughter in Whitechapel ended that night. Jack the Ripper never claimed another victim.

Niall MacGinnis, Robert Brown

Dorothy Alison, Niall MacGinnis

JACK THE RIPPER (1959)

DIRECTED BY ROBERT S. BAKER, MONTY BERMAN

CAST

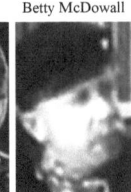

Lee Patterson..........................Sam Lowry
Eddie Byrne....................Inspector O'Neill
Betty McDowall.......................Anne Ford
Ewen Solon.....................Sir David Rogers
John Le Mesurier.....................Dr. Tranter
George Rose......................................Clarke
Philip Leaver............Music Hall Manager
Barbara Burke....................Kitty Knowles
Anne Sharp.......................................Helen
Denis Shaw.......................................Simes
Jack Allen....Asst. Commissioner Hodges
Jane Taylor..Hazel
Dorinda Stevens..........................Margaret
Hal Osmond...................................Snakey
George Street..................Station Sergeant
Olwen Brookes.......................Mrs. Bolton
Endre Muller..............................Louis Benz
Esma Cannon..................................Nelly
George Woodbridge.........................Blake
Bill Shine.....................Lord Tom Sopwith
Marianne Stone..............Drunken Woman
Garard Green.........................Dr. Urquhart
Charles Lamb..................................Harry
Jennifer White.....................................Beth
Cameron Hall....................Hospital Porter
Alan Robinson..............................Coroner
Anthony Sagar.................................Drunk

John Mott..............................Singer
Lucy Griffiths........SalvationArmy Woman
John Barrett...............................Onlooker
Katy Cashfield........................Blonde Girl
Helena Digby.........................First Victim
Paul Frees....................................Narrator

AND: Harold Coyne, Peter Diamond, Aidan Harrington, George Hilsdon, Ken Hutchins, Ned Lynch, Harry Phipps, Patricia Phoenix, Pat Ryan, George Schock, Ray Schock, Jack Silk, Harry Van Engel, Joe Wadham, June West

84 minutes

In London in 1888, a string of prostitute slayings by an elusive murderer known as "Jack The Ripper" leads conscientious Inspector O'Neill to assign all his men to solve the case.

Lobby Card

However, after weeks of futile police investigation, the distrustful public turns to accusing strangers of the crime, resulting in O'Neill's friend, visiting New York policeman Sam Lowry, being subjected to a fistfight at a local pub.

After O'Neill saves Sam from a beating, he agrees to allow the American to accompany him on the investigation. That evening, another woman is attacked by The Ripper, who asks, as he has done before, "Are you Mary Clarke?" before killing her.

Ewen Solon, Jack Allen

Lee Patterson looking serious

John Le Mesurier as Dr. Tranter

Gerard Green, Endre Muller, John Le Mesurier

Bill Shine, George Woodbridge, Philip Leaver

Just minutes after the murder, chief surgeon Dr. Tranter arrives late for his operation on patient Kitty Knowles at Mercy Hospital for Women.

The Ripper's victim is also sent to the hospital, where hospital governor Sir David Rogers performs an autopsy, concluding that, as with the other murders, the wounds are consistent with someone familiar with the medical profession.

Meanwhile, Tranter's ward, Anne Ford, has taken the position as head of hospital charity cases, even though Tranter disapproves of her work with the lower classes and dismisses the latest Ripper victim as another drab, unworthy of his time.

When Tranter and Anne try to leave the hospital that night, an angry mob attacks them, prompting O'Neill and Sam to quickly save them from harm.

The next day, Anne sadly admits that because the victims are of questionable background, she believes the deaths have been disregarded, and agrees to help retrace some of their last steps.

Tranter orders Anne to stop her association with the Sam but she ignores the advice and takes Sam to an East End nightclub that employed one of The Ripper's victims.

Jack Allen, Eddie Byrne

John Le Mesurier, Betty McDowall

After a crowd-pleasing can-can dance act, the dance hall manager sends new dancer Hazel, with veteran Margaret, to "entertain" two wealthy gentlemen in a private room. When one of the men molests Hazel, she flees the building. Dance hall worker Harry is sent after her and passes by a cloaked stranger, but does not find Hazel until after The Ripper has killed her. Outside the club, Anne and Sam find Tranter, who claims to have been following them and demands that Anne return home.

Ewen Solon, Betty McDowall

Eddie Byrne, Lee Patterson

Ewen Solon as Sir David Rogers

Sam goes to the scene of the crime, where an angry mob accuses the hospital's hunchbacked assistant, Louis Benz, of the crime after he drops his hospital bag filled with scalpels on the street.

As dozens of men corner Louis, O'Neill steps in to prevent them from stabbing the innocent man. Later, O'Neill places Louis in protective custody, despite the commissioner's and the public's conviction that he is guilty.

Lee Patterson, Ewen Solon, Eddie Byrne

Lee Patterson, George Rose, Eddie Byrne

Endre Muller as Louis Benz

When an infuriated Sir David tells the commissioner that his staff is required to carry medical tools and demands charges be dropped, the embarrassed commissioner relents. Later, O'Neill learns that Harry had overheard the cloaked stranger ask, "Is your name Mary Clarke?" just before Hazel's death.

O'Neill then finds Mary Clarke's father, who is unable to tell them where Mary is, but does reveal that a man carrying a doctor's bag asked for her location several months ago.

After Kitty is released from the hospital, Anne visits her at her apartment and learns that Kitty's fiancee, a prospective surgeon, committed suicide after learning of Kitty's promiscuous past.

Leaving the apartment, Anne hides when she suddenly suspects The Ripper is following her, but her footsteps alert Sir David, who finds Anne and claims to have been following her for her own protection.

Denis Shaw, Hal Osmond

Jane Taylor, George Woodbridge

Hal Osmond, Eddie Byrne

Later at the hospital, when Tranter shows disinterest in saving another drab, Louis protests and calls Sir David into the operating room to save the woman. Meanwhile, as Anne is transcribing the details from Kitty's birth certificate, she learns that the young woman's given name was Mary Clarke.

Tranter, disturbed by his own neglect of duties, offers his resignation to Sir David, who kindly suggests he take a vacation instead. That night, Anne returns to Kitty's apartment to deliver some food. Kitty is not there, and when Anne enters the pantry to store the food she is locked in by The Ripper.

Soon after, Kitty returns home and finds The Ripper waiting for her. When he calls her "Mary Clarke," Kitty admits her real identity, prompting him to accuse her of killing his son, who was engaged to Kitty, by turning a promising surgeon into a man obsessed with a "slut."

As he pulls out a scalpel from a medicine bag, Kitty struggles for her life, but she is killed. Realizing that the same fate awaits her, Anne barricades herself in the pantry.

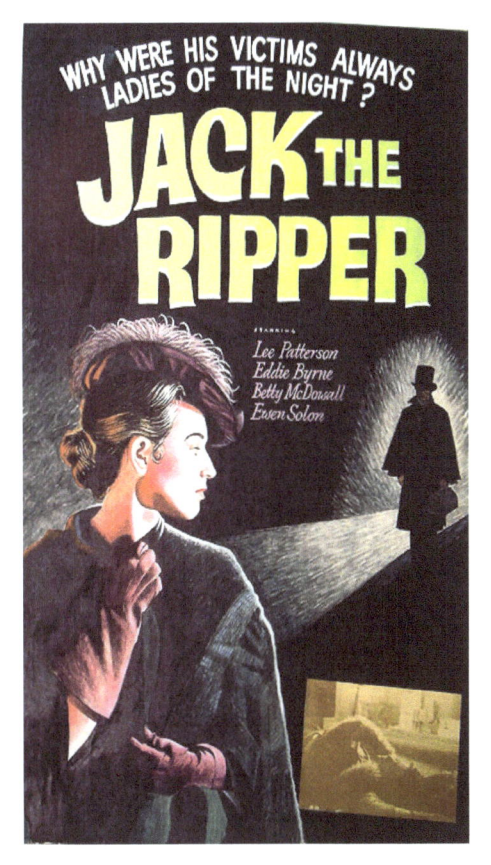

Film Poster

Film Poster

Meanwhile, Sam spots the birth certificate in Anne's office, rushes to Kitty's address and, hearing Anne's screams, breaks down the door. The Ripper flees out the window before he is seen.

Arriving at the hospital, Sir David stabs a guard who notices his bloody clothes. Sam rushes to the hospital with the doctor's bag belonging to the killer and tells Sir David that he believes The Ripper is in the hospital. O'Neill then attempts to trick Sir David into admitting to the murders by telling him that the guard is still alive and demanding that Sir David operate on him.

Fearing that the guard can identify him, Sir David escapes into the elevator shaft. While others search the building, two orderlies descend in the elevator to the ground floor with the guard's dead body, accidentally crushing Sir David to death . Later, O'Neill and Sam admit to Anne that because they cannot prove Sir David's guilt, the case will remain officially unsolved forever.

John Le Mesurier, Betty McDowall

Ewen Solon, Garard Green

Dorinda Stevens, Bill Shine

YOURS TRULY, JACK THE RIPPER SEASON 1 EPISODE 28

Directed By Ray Milland Original Air Date: 4/11/61

CAST

Boris Karloff	Host
John Williams	Sir Guy
Donald Woods	Dr. John Carmody
Edmon Ryan	Captain Pete Jago
Ottola Nesmith	Rowena
Adam Williams	Hymie Kralik
Nancy Valentine	Arlene
Ransom Sherman	Commissioner
Sam Gilman	Police Lieutenant
Ralph Clanton	Lester Baston
Jill Livesey	First Victim
Pamela Curran	Second Victim
Johnny Melfi	Artist
Gloria Blondell	Maggie Radevik
Art Lewis	Dr. Fisher
J. Pat O'Malley	Street Singer
Lillian O'Malley	Accordionist
Beverly Powers	Miss Beverly Hills
Chalky Williams	Policeman
Noble Chissell	Bystander
Joe Ploski	Mourner
Jimmie Horan	Artist
Mathew McCue	Pallbearer
Joseph La Cava	Waiter
George Ford, Shep Houghton	Club Patrons

J. Pat O'Malley   Lillian O'Malley   Policeman

In 1888 prostitute Mary Jane Kelly leaves a pub in London and walks home down the foggy streets. She sneaks past a policeman, turns a corner in the fog and bumps into another policeman. This constable tells her she knows better than to be out at night.-Jack The Ripper might be hiding in the shadows waiting for her. And indeed he is...

John Williams & Edmon Ryan

Edmon Ryan, Ransom Sherman

Johnny Melfi, John William, Ottola Nesmith

Television Poster

In New York in 1961, a series of murders comparable to the Jack the Ripper killings of 1888 is occurring. British Ripper expert Sir Guy is convinced that the murderer is not a copycat killer, but the Ripper himself, who has somehow found the formula to eternal youth. Sir Guy believes Jack is still alive, performing his grisly mission on a rhythmic cycle every three years and eight months. In addition, the locations of each murder wind up forming a sign that might provide a hint as to where the Ripper might strike next.

Captain Pete Jago is in charge of the investigation of the latest string of Jack the Ripper murders; he feels that Sir Guy is way off base, but as the Ripper murders continue exactly as Sir Guy predicted, Jago begins to give credence to Sir Guy's theories.

Donald Woods, John Williams

Adam Williams, Nancy Valentine, Johnny Melfi, John Williams

When Detective Jago says the natural process of life is to grow older, Sir Guy counters with the "unnatural" process of life. Sir Guy doesn't know whether Jack The Ripper kills to stay young or uses the stolen organs as demonic sacrifices.

After five murders, Sir Guy realizes he must catch the Ripper before the sixth and final killing. Then the Ripper will go on hiatus for three and a half years. Along with his friend and fellow police psychologist Dr. John Carmody, Sir Guy sets out to catch the Ripper.

Ottola Nesmith & Johnny Melfi

John Williams, Donald Woods

Donald Woods shows John Williams a knife

J. Pat O'Malley, Lillian O'Malley

Adam Williams at his easel

Problem is, Sir Guy miscalculated in thinking that the Ripper only killed women. Bad mistake. Sir Guy finally uncovers the Ripper, but unfortunately he turns out to be victim number six.

THE MONSTER OF LONDON CITY (1964)

DIRECTED BY EDWIN ZBONEK

CAST

Hansjorg Felmy....................Richard Sand
Marianne Koch......................Ann Morlay
Dietmar Schonherr.......Dr. Morley Greely
Hans Nielsen....................Inspector Dorne
Charklia Baxevanos..................Betty Ball
Peer Schmidt........................Teddy Flynn
Fritz Tillmann............Sir George Edwards
Walter Pfeil..................................Horrlick
Kurd Pieritz......................................Maylor
Elsa Wagner...............Housekeeper Emily
Kai Fischer........................Helen Capstick
Gudrun Schmidt................Evelyn Nichols
Adelhide Hinz..........................Maid Betsy
Christiane Schmidtmer........................Girl
Albert Bessler......................................Man
Manfred Grote..........................Detective
Gerda Blisse................................Assistant

AND: Walter Fein, Manfred Schuster, Ilse Stockl

90 minutes

The spirit of Jack the Ripper seems to be very much alive in 1960s London as a series of brutal slayings by the Monster of London City in the seedy Whitechapel neighborhood has Scotland Yard baffled.

In a macabre coincidence, a new play about the famous murderer is about to become a major West End hit. The play's leading man, Richard Sand, soon becomes the prime suspect.

Hans Nielsen, Dietmar Schonherr

Hans Nielsen, Dietmar Schonherr

Marianne Koch behind the bars

Sand is in love with Ann Morlay, who lives with her uncle and guardian Sir George Edwards, who happens to be a member of parliament. Sir George makes it clear that he much prefers young Dr. Greely, whom Anne has also been seeing.

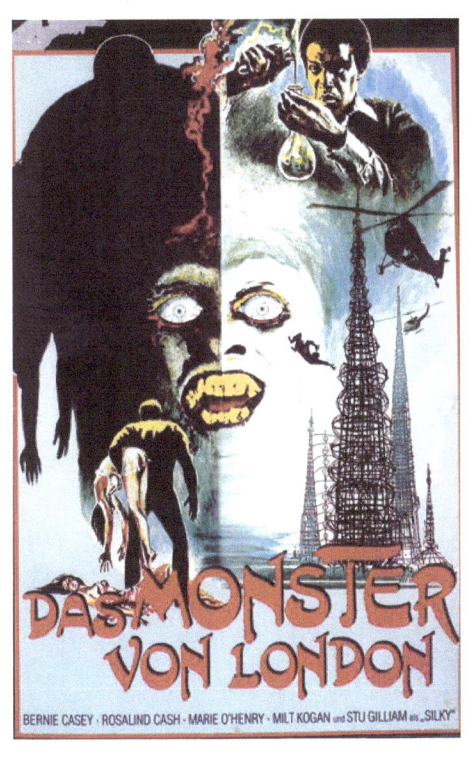

Film Poster

Film Poster

Dietmar Schonherr, Marianne Koch, Hansjorg Felmy, Walter Pfiel

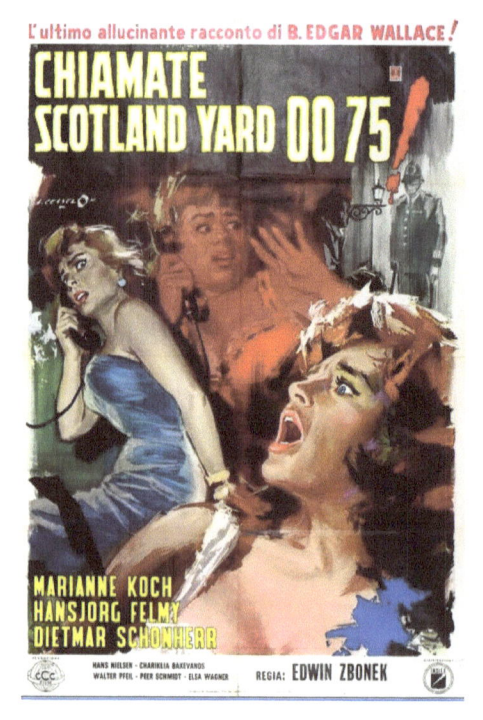

Film Poster   Policeman doing his work

Gudrun Schmidt, Dietmar Schonherr, Hans Nielsen

Sir George seems to be living something of a secret life, disappearing at night on mysterious errands that seem to coincide with the murders, sneaking out of his house through a secret passage. The Scotland Yard detective in charge of the investigation and sir George both violently disapprove of the play and blame it for the murders.

The producer of the play isn't worried as the murders have been great publicity and have boosted the box-office. Richard is starting to feel the pressure however and talks of abandoning the role. Meanwhile the murders just keep happening.

Woman chased through the fog

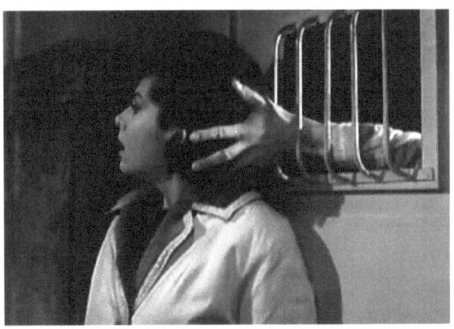

Marianne Koch menaced

Fritz Tillmann on the street

Sand becomes the police's prime suspect in the Whitechapel killings. Richard has a history of drug addiction and spent some time in a sanitarium. Furthermore, Richard begins having black-out spells instead of alibis as the murders occur.

It turns out to be a strange revenge from a man over the theft of his fiancee by another man who's involved in the play, and it all ends the same way the play does.

Hans Nielsen, Marianne Koch

Marianne Koch, Fritz Tillmann

Dietmar Schonherr with the bust

A STUDY IN TERROR (1965)

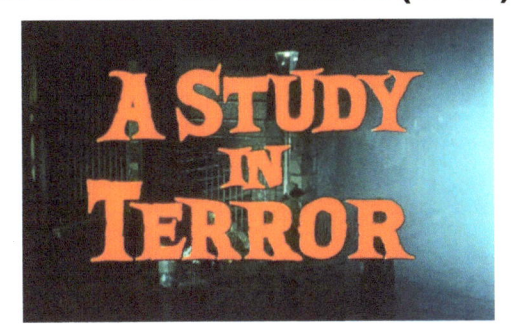

DIRECTED BY JAMES HILL

CAST

John Neville	Sherlock Holmes
Donald Houston	Dr. Watson
Robert Morley	Mycroft Holmes
John Fraser	Lord Carfax
Anthony Quayle	Dr. Murray
Adrienne Corri	Angela Osborne
Frank Finlay	Inspector Lestrade
Judi Dench	Sally Young
Cecil Parker	Prime Minister
Barry Jones	Duke of Shires
Kay Walsh	Catherine Eddowes
Edina Ronay	Mary Kelly
Norma Foster	Elizabeth Stride
Barbara Windsor	Annie Chapman
Christiane Maybach	Polly Nicholls
Dudley Foster	Home Secretary
Peter Carsten	Max Steiner
Georgia Brown	Singer
Charles Regnier	Joseph Beck
Barbara Leake	Mrs. Hudson
John Cairney	Michael Osborne
Avis Bunnage	Landlady
Patrick Newell	P.C. Benson
Terry Downes	Chunky
Jeremy Lloyd	Rupert
Corin Redgrave	Rupert's Friend
Sally Douglas	Blonde Whore in pub

Harriet Devine......Brunette Whore in pub
Donna White.........................Streetwalker
Eric Kent..Butcher
Joe Beckett......................Dick the Barman
Michael Collins..................................Man
Josie Grant.........................Whore in Pub
Jimmy Scott................................Passerby
Peter Diamond................................Sailor
Redmond Bailey, Emil Stemmler........Barmen
Richard Atherton, Cecil Paul, Roy Seeley.
....Butlers
Peter Hannon, Walter Henry, Mike Stevens....
....P.C.s
Bill Brandon, Billy Cornelius, Stan Simmons..Ruffians
Herman Cohen, Ernest C. Jennings, Gerry Judge, Rosalind Mendleson............
....People in Crowd
Robin Burns, Pat Donahue, Hilda Green, Colin McKenzie, George Oliver, Len Saunders, Fred Woods..................Beggars
David Baker, Del Baker, John Cam, Jimmy Charters, Ah Chong Choy, Billy Dean, Arthur Goodman, Richard Gregory, Sidney Gross, Colin McKenzie, Lou Morgan, Alec North, Johnny Rossi...........
....Pub Patrons

AND: Jack Armstrong, Bill Baskiville, Alan Beaton, Hyma Beckley, Alan Bennett, Ernest Blythe, Pauline Chamberlain, Mickey Clarke, Max Craig, Pamela Devereaux, Mo Dunster, Tommy Graham, Eric Henderson, Doreen Herrington, Jack Hetherington, Bill Hibbert, Ned Hood, Lew Hooper, Lindsay Hooper, Ken Hutchins, Tony Mendleson, John Moyce, Anne Munt, Peter Munt, Tony O'Leary, Dido Plumb, Charles Rayford, Bob E.

Raymond, Pat Ryan, John Scott, Sadie Slade, Hein Viljoen, Ron Watkins, Chris Webb, Philip Webb

| Cecil Paul | Roy Seeley | Peter Hannon |

| Walter Henry | Mike Stevens | Bill Brandon | Billy Cornelius | Stan Simmons | Ernest C. Jennings | Gerry Judge |

| Rosalind Mendleson | Pat Donahue | Colin McKenzie | George Oliver | Fred Woods | David Baker | Jimmy Charters |

| Ah Chong Choy | Richard Gregory | Colin McKenzie | Alec North | Johnny Rossi | Lew Hooper | Lindsay Hooper |

| Dido Plumb | Pat Ryan | Ron Watkins | George Hirste | Oliver Tomlin | Beggar 1 | Beggar 2 |

| Boy | Constable | Girl | Man 1 | Man 2 | Man 3 | Man 4 |

| Man 5 | Man 6 | Man 7 | Man 8 | Man 9 | Man 10 | Puppy |

83

Soldier 1 | Soldier 2 | Woman 1 | Woman 2 | Woman 3 | Woman 4 | Woman 5

Woman 6 | Woman 7 | Woman 8 | Woman 9 | Woman 10 | Woman 11 | Woman 12

Woman 13 | Woman 14 | Woman 15 | Woman 16

94 minutes

In London, England, in 1888, a streetwalker is brutally murdered in the Whitechapel area of the city. Patrons make merry in a local pub, the Angel and Crown, where a whore picks the pocket of a customer. Having been rumbled, she is thrown out by the pub owner, Max Steiner. "Nobody cheats the customers-except me," he says. This woman too becomes a victim of Jack the Ripper.

Donald Houston, John Neville

At the lodgings at 221b Baker Street, Dr. Watson is reading a newspaper article about Jack the Ripper. Holmes already has his own theory about the killer.

Back in Whitechapel, Annie Chapman may have had money to buy a new bonnet, but she doesn't have the small fee for her room, so the landlady turns her away. Annie becomes the Ripper's third victim.

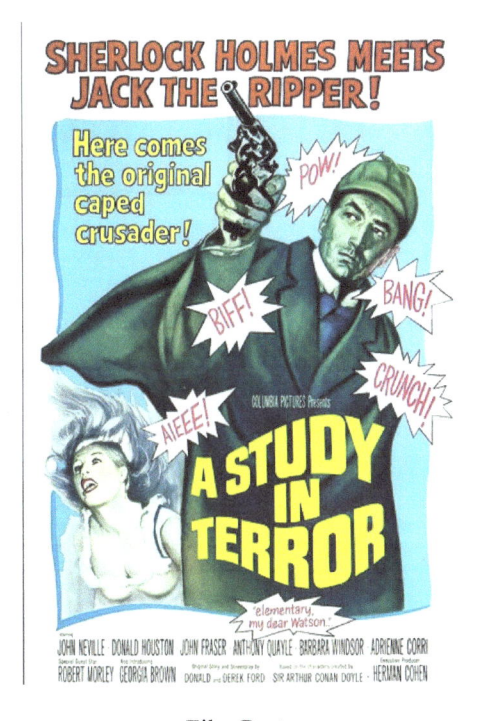

Film Poster

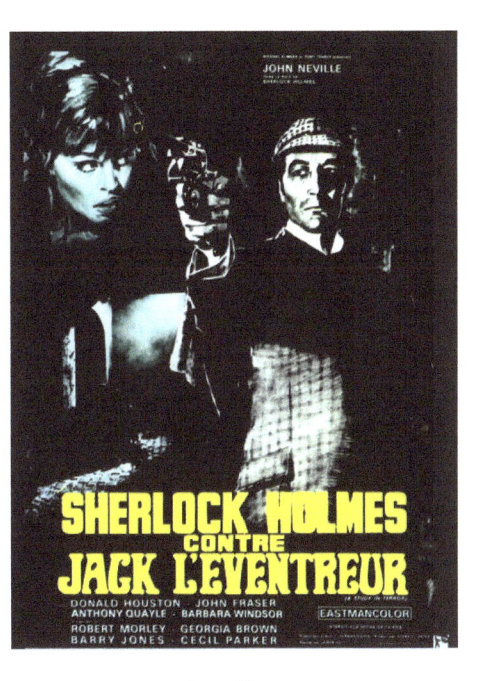

Foreign Film Poster

Robert Morley, Donald Houston, John Neville

The newspapers report the police are baffled. Holmes receives a parcel in the post, sent from Whitechapel by whom Holmes correctly deduces was a woman. The parcel contains a case of medical instruments-minus the large scalpel.

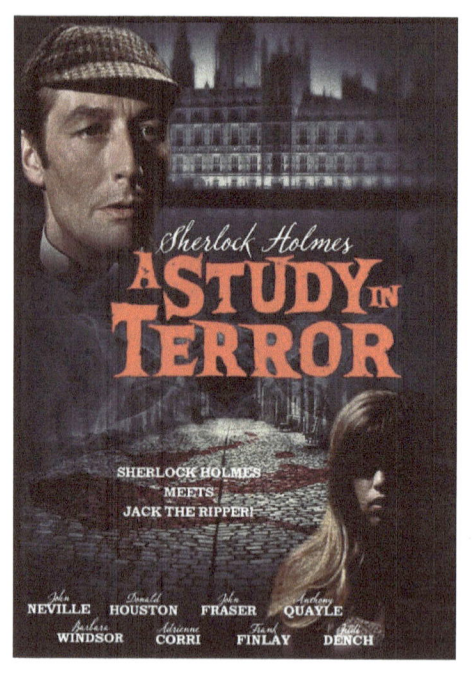

He realizes that the case had been in a Whitechapel pawn shop, in a narrow street facing South. He also can tell the pawnbroker is foreign, by the way he wrote the number seven on the case in chalk. A crest on the case lead Holmes and Watson to the Duke of Shires, who tells Holmes that the medical case belonged to his son, Michael Osborne, now deceased.

Film Poster

Judi Dench, John Fraser

John Neville, Donald Houston

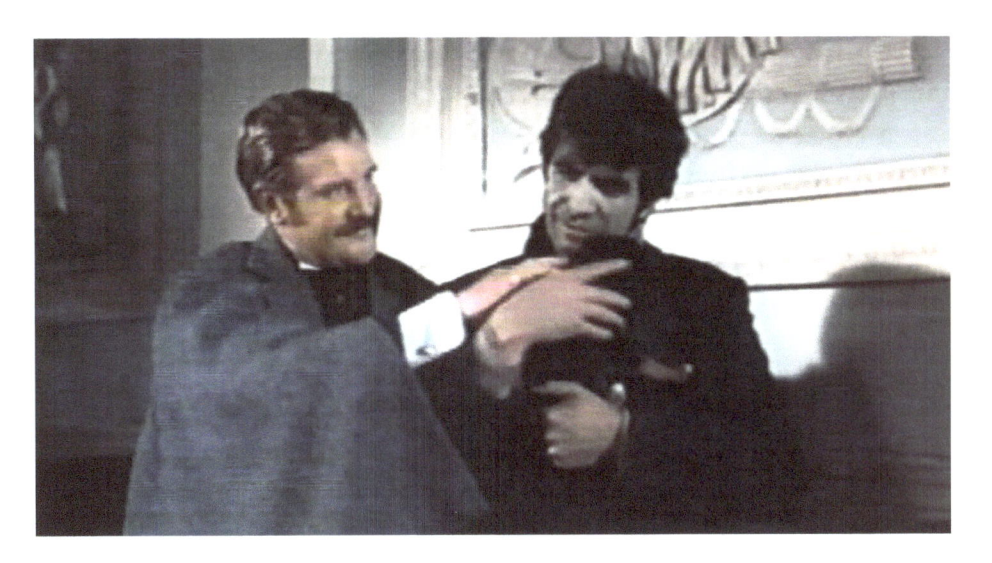

Donald Houston, John Cairney & Puppy

Donald Houston, John Neville

On the way out, Holmes meets the Duke's other son, Edward, Lord Carfax, who confirms that the case did in fact belong to his brother. Travelling to Whitechapel in search of the pawnshop, Holmes and Watson come upon a shop owned by Joseph Beck, a foreign gentleman, as Holmes had said. Beck tells him the case was pawned by a lady called Angela Osborne, but that was two years ago. Her address at the time was an East End hostel, more or less a soup kitchen, run by Dr. Murray. Holmes is convinced that there is a connection between the case of medical instruments and the Jack the Ripper murders.

He asks Inspector Lestrade to allow him to examine the body of Annie Chapman, the most recent victim. Dr. Murray has performed the autopsy, and upon examination agrees with Holmes that two weapons were used-a scalpel and a bayonet. One weapon indicates a doctor, the other a soldier, but Holmes thinks the bayonet was used to cover up the knife wounds. He tells Lestrade to forget about soldiers, and look for someone living alone in or near Whitechapel-a person with some surgical skill.

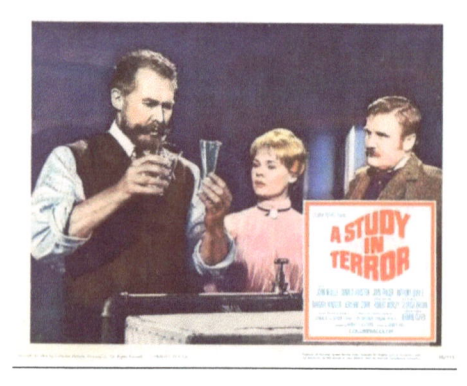

Lobby Card

John Neville, Donald Houston

Donald Houston, Frank Finlay

Anthony Quayle, John Neville

Frank Finlay, John Neville

On the instructions of Holmes, Watson goes to the hostel next day to inquire about Angela Osborne. Holmes has told him to make quite a scene, and the result is that Sally Young-a volunteer at the hostel, immediately runs off after Watson leaves. Holmes has forseen this; he was disguised a a tramp singing for his supper. He follows Sally a few streets away-she leads him to none other than Lord Carfax. Carfax then relates to Holmes the tragic story of his brother Michael, having married Angela, who had been a prostitute.

Angela had then attempted to blackmail the family with the assistance of Max Steiner-whose payoff was the Angel and Crown pub. In black tie and tails, Holmes and Watson visit the pub in question, where Steiner tells them he knows nothing of Angela Osborne.

Holmes knows that he's lying, but decides to do nothing for the time being. As they are walking down a street outside the pub, Holmes and Watson are set upon and attacked by several thugs, who they manage to put to flight.

Barbara Windsor, Kay Walsh

Cecil Parker, Dudley Foster

Robert Morley, Donald Houston, John Neville, Frank Finlay

"Nothing like a piece of cold steel, eh?" says Watson. A few streets away, PC Benson moves another prostitute along; a few minutes later the woman becomes another Ripper victim. The press is in a fit again; Dr. Murray makes a speech to a crowd, whipping the people into a frenzy.

At 10 Downing Street the Prime Minister has called in Mycroft Holmes, Sherlock's elder brother, in order that the senior Holmes might use his influence to get Sherlock to finally bring down the Ripper- before the government is brought down.

John Neville, Robert Morley

Peter Carsten, Christiane Maybach

Holmes arrives at the mortuary where Dr. Murray is examining the latest victim. "Anyone with a modicum of medical training could have done it," Murray tells Holmes. Holmes suspects the missing Michael Osborne, but Murray keeps insisting Michael could not have anything to do with the killings.

Robert Morley has a cocktail

Robert Morley, Barry Jones

Patrick Newell, Norma Foster

Meanwhile Mary Kelly becomes the fifth Ripper victim. Inspector Lestrade tells Holmes that in this murder "You've never seen anything like it this side of hell." Holmes is finally able to track down the elusive Angela Osborne, as well as Michael, now a pathetic imbecile.

93

He returns Michael to his home with the Duke, who relents and forgives and takes his son back into the house. Realizing that Michael's condition makes it impossible for him to be the Ripper, Holmes deduces the fiend's true identity, setting a trap for him at the pub.

During a horrific fight, Angela, Max, and Jack the Ripper are killed as the pub burns to the ground. Holmes narrowly escapes, and London has no more to fear from the notorious Jack the Ripper.

John Neville, Donald Houston

John Neville, Donald Houston

John Fraser as Lord Carfax

HANDS OF THE RIPPER (1971)

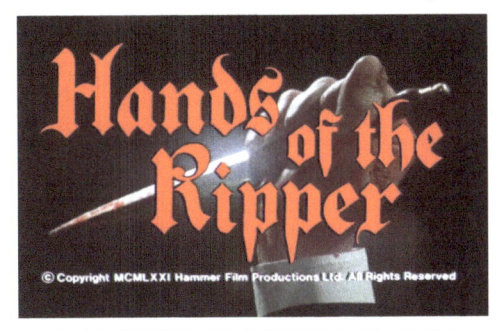

DIRECTED BY PETER SASDY

CAST

Eric Porter	Dr. John Pritchard
Angharad Rees	Anna
Jane Merrow	Laura
Keith Bell	Michael Pritchard
Derek Godfrey	Dysart
Dora Bryan	Mrs. Golding
Marjorie Rhodes	Mrs. Bryant
Lynda Baron	Long Liz
Marjie Lawrence	Dolly
Margaret Rawlings	Madame Bullard
Barry Lowe	Mr. Wilson
Elizabeth MacLennon	Mrs. Wilson
Norman Bird	Police Inspector
A.J. Brown	Reverend Anderson
April Wilding	Catherine
Ann Way	Seamstress
Peter Munt	Pleasants
Philip Ryan	P.C.
Molly Weir	Maude-Maid
Charles Lamb	Guard
Alex Lewis	Diner
Dido Plumb	Tramp
Danny Lyons	Jack the Ripper
Nadine Stapleton	Little Anna
Jack Armstrong	Gentleman
Jack Arrow	Browning
Pauline Chamberlain	Train Commuter

Max Craig...................................Prisoner
Terry Sartain......................Wedding Guest
Anne Clune, Josie Grant, Vicki Woolf......
....Cell Whores
Beulah Hughes, Tallulah Miller, Katya Wyeth......................................Pub Whores

AND: Richard Atherton, Roy Beck, Hugh Cecil, Jack Dearlove, Peter Diamond, Edward Eddon, Russell Forehead, Eden Fox, Alan Gibbs, Dave Griffiths, Lew Hooper, Fran Hunter, Ken Hutchins, Juba Kennerley, Tommy Little, Anne Munt, Tony O'Leary, Bob E. Raymond, Ray Schock, Jack Sharp, Reg Thomason, Mike Varey

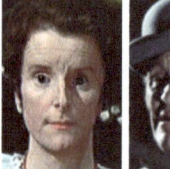

Ann Way  | Peter Munt  | Philip Ryan
Molly Weir  | Charles Lamb  | Alex Lewis 
Dido Plumb  | Danny Lyons | Nadine Stapleton 
Jack Armstrong  | Jack Arrow  | Max Craig 
Terry Sartain  | Anne Clune  | Vicki Woolf  | Beulah Hughes  | Tallulah Miller  | Katya Wyeth  | Richard Atherton 
Roy Beck  | Eden Fox  | Dave Griffiths  | Lew Hooper  | Fran Hunter | Juba Kennerley  | Tommy Little 
Bob E. Raymond  | Ray Schock  | Jack Sharp  | Reg Thomason  | Mike Varey

85 minutes

An angry mob chases a cloaked figure through the cobbled streets of Whitechapel, shouting "It's the Ripper!" The Ripper arrives home and then stabs his wife to death. This scene is witnessed by the couple's small daughter. Years later, the daughter has now grown into a beautiful young woman, who is seen hiding behind a grate in a parlour, giving voice to people's ghostly relatives.

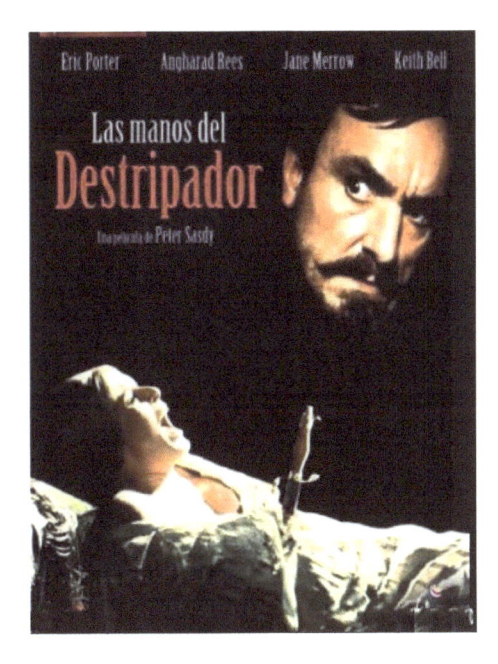

Film Poster

Foreign Film Poster

Derek Godfrey & Eric Porter

At the latest seance is a Dr. Pritchard, who ascertains the séance is rigged, and confronts Mrs. Golding, the fake medium. Anna, the girl, not only helps Mrs. Golding with her bogus tricks, but also entertains clients upstairs.

When Anna's latest customer flashes some jewelry at her, it sends the girl into a trance. The man, Dysart, begins slapping Anna, and when Mrs. Golding intervenes, she is impaled on the door by a poker.

Philip Ryan, Norman Bird, Derek Godfrey

Eric Porter, Derek Godfrey

Angharad Rees, Dora Bryan

Dr. Pritchard provides Dysart with an alibi-even though he is not responsible for the crime-and then goes to the lunatic asylum where Anna has been taken and removes her, bringing her back with him to his own home.

"I'm going to look after you from now on," Pritchard tells Anna. "Would you like that? All you have to do is learn to become one of the family."

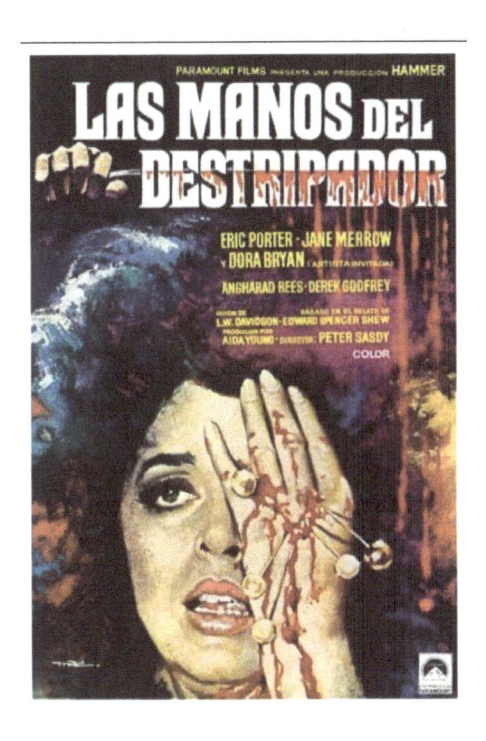

Foreign Film Poster

Film Poster

Jane Merrow, Keith Bell

Angharad Rees, Eric Porter

Pritchard knows that Anna is the murderer, but being a recent convert to the teachings of Freud, he reckons he can figure out what motivates her behavior. And if a few maids and prostitutes get massacred in the process, they've sacrificed their lives in the name of psychology. All this despite being told by Dysart that during the murder, "her hands-they weren't her hands at all!"

Film Poster

Marjorie Rhodes, Eric Porter

Eric Porter, Keith Bell

Anna then embarks on a killing spree, each explosion of blood-splashing violence sparked off by either shiny objects or kisses on the cheek. First to be murdered by Anna is Pritchard's maid, Dolly, who's a lovely girl.

After finding the poor young maid with her neck gaping wide open and covered in stab wounds, Pritchard prescribes rest and care for the troubled Anna.

Eric Porter finds a body

Angharad Rees, Eric Porter

Keith Bell, Jane Merrow, Eric Porter

Elizabeth MacLennan, Barry Lowe

The next to feel the wrath of a now-hypnotized Anna is a prostitute named Long Liz who kindly takes her in. Random acts of kindness don't help Anna, who stabs a woman with a handful of hat pins which actually go through her hand and into her eye.

Dysart warns Pritchard that "You can't cure Jack The Ripper-and that's who she is!" Finally, Anna stabs Pritchard with a ceremonial sword, then runs off. Pritchard hails a cab and follows Anna to the whispering gallery at St. Paul's Cathedral, where the final denouement takes place.

Margaret Rawlings, Angharad Rees

Marjorie Rhodes, A.J. Brown

French Lobby Card

JACK THE RIPPER

THE FIRST TWO EPISODE 1

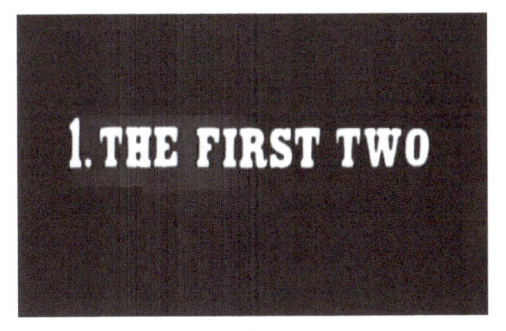

1. THE FIRST TWO

DIRECTED BY Leonard Lewis ORIGINAL AIR DATE: 7/13/73

CAST

Stratford Johns...Det. Chief Supt. Charles Barlow
Frank Windsor.....Det Chief Supt. John Watt
Kenneth Thornett................P.C. John Neil
Bryan Coleman....Dr. Rees Ralph Llewellyn
Alan Cullen...Dr. George Bagster Phillips
Frank Duncan.....................Wynne Baxter
Stanley Dawson.................Jury Chairman
Varley Thomas...................Emily Holland
Freda Dowie......................Amelia Palmer
Chris Gannon...............Timothy Donovan

Chris Fenwick..................John Richardson
Hugo De Vernier...............Albert Cadosch
Rosalind Ross....................Elizabeth Long
Gabrielle Hamilton.....Amelia Richardson
Wendy Williams....................Mrs. Barnett
Desmond Jordan.................Charles Booth
Lewis Wilson............................Pub Patron
Patrick Jordan......................Police Officer
Julie May..........................Mrs. Fiddymont
Velvey Attwood.................Mary Chappell
Peter Spraggon..........................Policeman
Geoffrey Todd....Sergeant William Thicke
Gordon Christie....Inspector Frederick Abberline
Jean Hilton........................Elizabeth Stride
Victor Croxford.........................Pub Patron
Ernest Blythe, Ernest C. Jennings, Colin Thomas...............................Jury Members
John Beardmore, Bob E. Raymond, Philip Stewart..............................Press Reporters

Stanley Dawson — Varley Thomas — Freda Dowie
Chris Gannon — Chris Fenwick — Hugo De Vernier
Rosalind Ross — Gabrielle Hamilton — Wendy Williams
Desmond Jordan — Lewis Wilson — Patrick Jordan
Julie May — Velvey Attwood — Peter Spraggon — Geoffrey Todd — Gordon Christie — Ernest Blythe — Ernest C. Jennings
Juror

Barlow and Watt decide to take a look at the case of Jack the Ripper, which occurred 85 years beforehand. Barlow comments that eight inspectors were on the case.

They begin by concentrating on the victims in order; Polly Nichols was the first. Dr. Rees Ralph Llewellyn conducted the post mortem, and gave lengthy testimony at the inquest.

104

P.C. Neil discovered the body, and gave evidence. Before the inquest is concluded, another woman, Annie Chapman, is murdered. Dr. George Bagster Phillips is called in this time. He thinks that justice may be thwarted if all the evidence is made public.

Barlow and Watt go over more evidence, including testimony from witnesses who saw the first two victims not too long before they were murdered. A giant chart is used to collate the information.

Barlow goes over the names on the board

Frank Duncan, Alan Cullen

Frank Windsor, Stratford Johns

Frank Windsor, Stratford Johns

Jury listens at the inquest

Wendy Williams, Desmond Jordan

105

They also get an idea of just what appalling conditions the people of Whitechapel and Spitalfields lived in during 1888. Poverty and filth were the order of the day.

Barlow concludes that Inspector Abberline, who was in charge of the investigation, was looking for a down-and-out type, which he thinks was wrong. Watt is interested in the ritual nature of the killings.

Policeman discovers a body

Julie May in the pub

Frank Windsor, Stratford Johns

Alan Cullen at the inquest

DOUBLE EVENT EPISODE 2

2: DOUBLE EVENT

DIRECTED BY Gilchrist Calder ORIGINAL AIR DATE: 7/20/73

CAST

Stratford Johns...Det. Chief Supt. Charles Barlow
Frank Windsor.....Det Chief Supt. John Watt
Gabor Vernon...............Louis Diemschutz
Jean Hilton.......................Elizabeth Stride
Malcolm Hayes........................John Kelly
Anthony Woodruff...............Mr. Crawford
Robert Tayman...........................Coroner
Norman Henry............Major Henry Smith
Bill Ward..........................Michael Kidney
Basil Henson...............Sir Charles Warren
Frank Duncan.....................Wynne Baxter
Geoffrey Rose.....................Dr. Blackwell
Hilary Sesta................Catherine Eddowes
Brian Badcoe.....Dr. Frederick Gordon Brown
Kenneth Keeling...................George Lusk
Alan Cullen...Dr. George Bagster Phillips
John Rolfe......Det. Sergeant Daniel Halse
George Raistrick.............Joseph Lawende
Allan McClelland.....Dr. Robert Anderson
Lane Meddick...........Editor of The Strand
Alfred Maron................................Witness
Eric Mason................................P.C. Lamb
Maurice O'Connell.....P.C. William Smith
Alan Downer..................P.C. Alfred Long
Aldwyn Davies..................Press Reporter

Eden Fox, John Hughman, Terry Martin, John Timberlake, Graham Tonbridge........
....Jurors
Stenson Falcke, Noel Flanagan, Tony O'Leary, Christopher Webb, Lincoln Wright
....Men in Court
Peter Childs, Robert Mill, Stanley Price, Allen Sykes...P.C.s

John Rolfe   George Raistrick   Allan McClelland

Lane Meddick   Alfred Maron   Eric Mason

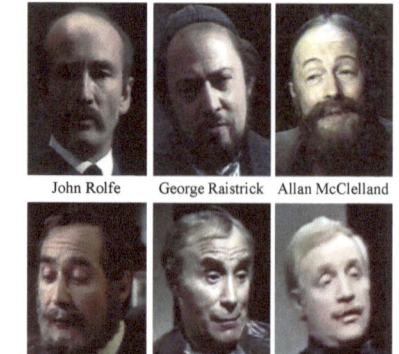

Maurice O'Connell   Alan Downer   Graham Tonbrige   Noel Flanagan   Peter Childs   Robert Mill   Stanley Price

Allen Sykes   Man 1   Man 2   Man 3   Man 4   Man 5   Office Boy

On September 30th, 1888, Jack the Ripper struck twice; murdering both Elizabeth Stride and Catherine Eddowes. This later became known as the "Double Event." Barlow and Watt examine the evidence.

Louis Diemschutz discovered the first body, that of Elizabeth Stride, at number 40 Berner Street when coming home with his pony and trap. The next victim, Catherine Eddowes, was found by a policeman in Mitre Square.

Alan Cullen, Frank Duncan

Frank Windsor, Stratford Johns

Witnesses give evidence at the inquest on the two women, as to their whereabouts and movements on the day preceding their murders. Nothing unusual or startling is revealed.

A number of policemen give evidence, as well as some doctors who examined the remains. Doctors Blackwell and Frederick Gordon Brown give extensive medical evidence.

Following these murders, the Whitechapel Vigilance Committee was formed, headed by George Lusk. Watt says that Lusk probably enjoyed reading his name in the papers.

Gabor Vernon as Diemschutz

TV Poster

Frank Windsor, Stratford Johns

Men at the inquest

Inquest scene

Stanley Price giving testimony

Barlow points at the map

Anthony Woodruff et al

Barlow is astonished to hear that someone-a senior police officer-ordered that a chalked message found on a wall in Goulston Street was rubbed out before it could be photographed.

Barlow goes on to say that it could very well have been written by Jack the Ripper, and to rub it out was destroying evidence. Turns out that Police Commissioner Sir Charles Warren ordered it rubbed off.

BUTCHERY EPISODE 3

3: BUTCHERY

DIRECTED BY David Wickes ORIGINAL AIR DATE: 7/27/73

CAST

Stratford Johns...Det. Chief Supt. Charles Barlow
Frank Windsor.....Det Chief Supt. John Watt
Brian Badcoe.....Dr. Frederick Gordon Brown
Alan Cullen...Dr. George Bagster Phillips
Ernest Claydon......................John Bowyer
Johnny Shannon.................John McCarthy
Eammon Boyce...................Joseph Barnett
Mark Eden................................Journalist
Jessie Robins..................Catherine Pickett
Rose Hiller.........................Mary Ann Cox
Norman Scace...Dr. Roderick MacDonald
Geoffrey Lumsden......Daily Telegraph Editor
Hal Jeayes..................George Hutchinson
Margaret Brady................Elizabeth Prater
Lewis Wilson...Commercial St. Detective
Mollie Maureen.................Queen Victoria
Norman Henry............Major Henry Smith
Allan McClelland.....Dr. Robert Anderson
Norman Shelley......Detective Constable Dew
Anthony Woodruff..............Mr. Crawford
Mary Quinn...................Caroline Maxwell
Caroline Citroen.............Mary Jane Kelly
Nadim Sawalha...........Ghoulish Onlooker
Margaret Pilleau.............Ghoulish Mother
Juba Kennerley.................Inquest Official
Harry Tierney.......................................P.C.

111

Walter Goodman.................Man at Inquest
Leslie Bryant, Eden Fox, Keith James, Ronald Nunnery, Bryan Poyser, Charles Rayford, Graham Tonbridge, Garth Watkins..Jurors

Mollie Maureen   Norman Henry   Allan McClelland

Norman Shelley   Anthony Woodruff   Mary Quinn

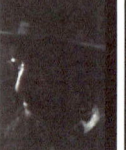

Nadim Sawalha   Margaret Pilleau   Juba Kennerley   Keith James   Bryan Poyser   Charles Rayford   Infant

Man   Woman

Barlow and Watt discuss the case of Mary Kelly, the final Ripper victim. Barlow remarks that there was a gap of 40 days since the double event of Stride and Eddowes on September 30th. Watt however wants to go back to the Catherine Eddowes killing, and the writing on the wall. He points out that "Juwes" was spelled a particular way.

Norman Scace questions a witness

Onlookers at the grisly crime scene

He then points out that the Masons may have been involved, as this word means Jubela, Jubelo, and Jubelum, three architects of the temple of King Solomon, who murdered Grand Master Hiram Abiff.

Returning to the grisly murder of Mary Kelly-the only victim killed indoors-landlord John McCarthy dispatches John Bowyer to Miller's Court to collect the rent Mary Kelly owed. She was way behind. Bowyer finds something he will never forget.

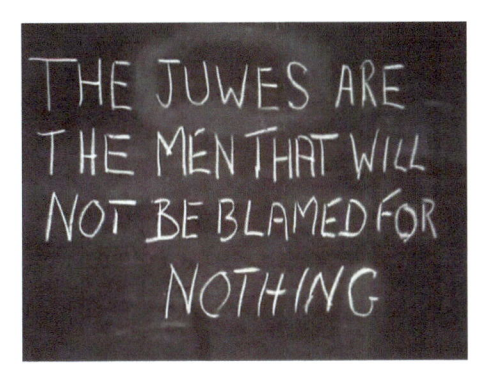

Chalked writing on the Goulston Street wall

Jurors include Charles Rayford and Juba Kennerley

Johnny Shannon, Ernest Claydon

Dr. Roderick MacDonald conducts the inquest; some of the jurors begin complaining that they are from other districts, but MacDonald will tolerate no nonsense.

Barlow thinks it odd that there was nothing about the time of death or the many injuries to Kelly's body brought up at the inquest. The medical testimony of Dr. Phillips was extremely terse.

Watt tells Barlow to go and get the official files on the case, but Barlow says they will not to be open until 1993-that's 20 years down the road. But Barlow will try and pull some strings.

Eammon Boyce giving evidence

Stratford Johns, Frank Windsor

Jurors listen at the inquest

Entrance to Miller's Court

Frank Windsor, Stratford Johns

114

PANIC EPISODE 4

4: PANIC

DIRECTED BY Leonard Lewis ORIGINAL AIR DATE: 8/3/73

CAST

Stratford Johns...Det. Chief Supt. Charles Barlow
Frank Windsor.....Det Chief Supt. John Watt
Basil Henson...............Sir Charles Warren
John Law.........................Henry Matthews
Alan Foss................................J. Ponsford
Peter Gray................Sir Augustus Padgett
Derek Birch...........................Mr. Nimmo
John Malcolm.......................E.K. Larkins
Allan McClelland.....Dr. Robert Anderson
Gordon Christie....Inspector Frederick Abberline
Frank Duncan.....................Wynne Baxter
Kenneth Keeling...................George Lusk
Norman Shelley......Detective Constable Dew
Geoffrey Lumsden......Daily Telegraph Editor
Mollie Maureen.................Queen Victoria
Eric Dodson...Pembroke Square Letter Writer
Will Stampe..............................Star Editor
Alan Ford............................Star Reporter
David Scase.......................Star Columnist
Stuart Latham...................Sydney Oswald
Sonnie Willis..................Private Secretary
Ernest Blythe, Richard Simpson......Jurors
Vernon Duke, Charlie Gray, Fred Machon, Laurie Rose, Terry Sartain..............
....Meeting Attendees

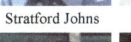

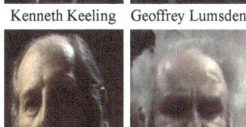

Alan Ford | David Scase | Stuart Latham | Sonnie Willis | Richard Simpson | Charlie Gray | Terry Sartain

Boy 1 | Boy 2 | G. Lee Pemberton | Man 1 | Man 2 | Man 3 | Star Employee

Woman

By the end 1888, the East End slums were up in arms and there was a fear that rioting could spill over to the wealthier areas of London. Barlow and Watt look into what was said and done and whether Jack the Ripper was a Mason.

Barlow has had a look at the sealed files; in it, he finds a letter written by Sir Charles Warren, explaining his decision to have the chalked message found on the wall in Goulston Street erased.

Will Stampe and friend

Numerous letters are read and discussed by Barlow and Watt; most of them are to and from government dignitaries. Barlow and Watt take them all with a grain of salt.

A question of a reward came up during the Ripper atrocities; there are many different views about it. George Lusk feels that had a reward been offered early on, Jack the Ripper would have been caught.

However, the practice of offering rewards had been discontinued in 1884, after a dynamite conspiracy was uncovered. An innocent person was framed by the perpetrators.

Will Stampe and colleagues

Stuart Latham reads a letter

Sonnie Willis, Basil Henson

Barlow and Watt then go over all the letters received, allegedly written by Jack the Ripper, and try to determine which ones may be genuine. The police at the time received great criticism from the public.

After further review, Barlow tells Watt, "Well, with the mobs out of the way, perhaps detection can start." Watt says "Do you think we can place his name?"

Alan Ford, Will Stampe

Alan Ford, Will Stampe

Watt points to the board for Barlow

Contemporary drawing of a suspect

Frank Windsor, Stratford Johns

Frank Windsor, Stratford Johns

SUSPECTS EPISODE 5

DIRECTED BY Gilchrist Calder ORIGINAL AIR DATE: 8/10/73

CAST

Stratford Johns...Det. Chief Supt. Charles Barlow
Frank Windsor.....Det Chief Supt. John Watt
Terry Bale........................Henry Winslade
Alan Chuntz...................Montague Druitt
Christopher Benjamin.................Clubman
Maurice O'Connell.....P.C. William Smith
Frank Duncan......................Wynne Baxter
Hal Jeayes...................George Hutchinson
Cyril Shaps.................Dr. Thomas Dutton
Julian Somers..............William Le Queux
David Neal.......................Russian Official
Mary Quinn..................Caroline Maxwell
Norman Scace...Dr. Roderick MacDonald
Anne Blake...................Hermione Dudley
Christopher Burgess.............Sun Reporter
Leslie Sands.......Sir Melville Macnaghten
Kenneth Colley......................................P.C.
Gary Waldhorn...................William Druitt
Robert Sansom.....Dr. Thomas B. Diplock
Ginette McDonald..Australian Researcher
Gordon Christie....Inspector Frederick Abberline

Leslie Sands    Kenneth Colley    Gary Waldhorn    Robert Sansom    Ginette McDonald    Reporter

Barlow and Watt attempt to go through a wide range of suspects to determine the identity of Jack the Ripper. Watt remarks the main thing is that the killer had a great working knowledge of anatomy.

A London clubman in the 19th Century tells the story that a Dr. Howard exposed the Ripper as a prominent West End doctor, but all who knew about it were sworn to secrecy.

Anne Blake tells her story

Cyril Shaps telling his story

Leslie Sands as Macnaughten

The man goes on to say that the real credit for unmasking Jack the Ripper went to Robert James Lees, who early in his life was blessed with a clairvoyant power.

Back with Barlow and Watt, they read accounts of descriptions of various men seen with or near the victims at around the times of the murders. Abberline likes George Chapman as a suspect.

Frank Windsor, Stratford Johns

Stratford Johns, Frank Windsor

Frank Windsor as Watt

In an official document written by Sir Melville Macnaughten in 1894, he states that he knows the identity of Jack the Ripper, but for the safety of the man's relatives, he will not tell the name.

Macnaughten goes on to say that the Whitechapel murderer had five victims, and only five. The fury of the killer's mutilations increased with every case, culminated by the murder of Mary Kelly inside her room in Miller's Court.

According to Macnaughten, the killer's brain gave way after the final murder, and he committed suicide. Or alternatively, his relatives had him committed to an asylum. Barlow and Watt consider this.

Boys fished from the Thames

Terry Bale, Robert Sansom

Stratford Johns, Frank Windsor

David Neal reads a letter

THE HIGHEST IN THE LAND EPISODE 6

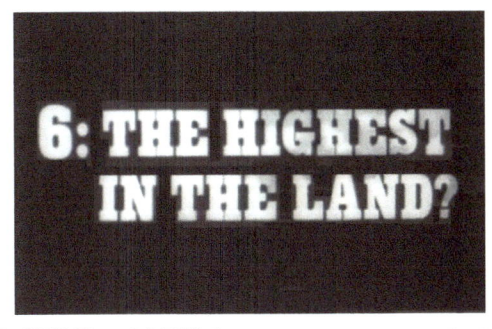

DIRECTED BY David Wickes ORIGINAL AIR DATE: 8/17/73

CAST

Stratford Johns...Det. Chief Supt. Charles Barlow
Frank Windsor.Det Chief Supt. John Watt
Sean Caffrey..........................Ernest Parke
Morris Perry...........................Lord Euston
Frank Gatliff...............Sir Charles Russell
Bernard Kay............................Lockwood
John Cazabon.........Sir Thomas Chambers
Simon Cuff................................John Saul
Christopher Benjamin.................Clubman
Norman Henry............Major Henry Smith
Frank Duncan......................Wynne Baxter
Hal Jeayes..................George Hutchinson
Leslie Sands.......Sir Melville Macnaghten
Rosalind Ross...................Elizabeth Long
Eammon Boyce.................Joseph Barnett
Maurice O'Connell.....P.C. William Smith
Michael Halsey........................P.C. Hanks
Lewis Wilson.......Cleveland St. Detective
Joseph Sickert...............................Himself
Roy Pattison, Harry Tierney..............P.C.s

123

Michael Halsey | Lewis Wilson | Joseph Sickert | Roy Pattison | Barrister 1 | Barrister 2 | Barrister 3

Court Policeman | Court Spectator | Duke of Clarence | George Chapman | M.J. Druitt | Princess Alexandra | Sir William Gull

Barlow and Watt begin this segment by going out into the East End of London, and exploring the murder sites. They remark that little has changed in the past 85 years.

Dr. Thomas Stowell wrote a letter that was published in 1970, which was picked up by 3,000 newspapers around the world. Although he does not name names, the theory is he accused Queen Victoria's grandson.

Morris Perry, Frank Gatliff

Stratford Johns, Frank Windsor

Sean Caffrey, Bernard Kay

Frank Windsor, Stratford Johns

124

There's a testimony by Joseph Sickert, who claims to be the illegitimate son of noted painter Walter Sickert. Sickert says that his father had told him a story that implicated not only the royal family but also a host of other famous people in the Jack the Ripper murders.

According to Sickert, Royal Physician Sir William Gull committed the murders with the help of accomplices. Barlow says that the mere belief of Joseph Sickert is not evidence.

Watt comes up with some documents that at least prove that Sickert's mother was who he says she was. The name of the father was left blank on the birth certificate.

Hal Jeayes makes a statement

Mitre Square street sign

Stratford Johns, Frank Windsor

John Cazabon as the judge

Christopher Benjamin as a clubman

Michael Halsey, Roy Pattison, Lewis Wilson

Nearing the end of the road, Barlow thinks that there was a cover-up. But Watt says he has never found it very easy to believe in conspiracies. But the Director of Public Prosecutions has a file that may hold the answer.

When Barlow went there, he was shown a file consisting of three pages. It was clear to him pages were removed. An official told Barlow that he should see some of the names on the papers he wasn't allowed to see!

KOLCHAK: THE NIGHT STALKER-THE RIPPER EPISODE 1

DIRECTED BY Allen Baron ORIGINAL AIR DATE: 9/13/74

CAST

Darren McGavin..................Carl Kolchak
Simon Oakland..................Tony Vincenzo
Ken Lynch........................Captain Warren
Beatrice Colen......................Jane Plumm
Ruth McDevitt............................Old Lady
Jack Grinnage.......................Ron Updyke
Marya Small..............................Masseuse
Robert Berger..............................Mailboy
Roberta Collins...................Det. Cortazzo
Clint Young.....................................Driver
Mickey Gilbert.......................The Ripper
Donald Mantooth.....................Policeman
Denise Dillaway.................Debbie Fielder
Cathy Paine.......................................Ellen
Eddie Garrett..........................Bus Driver
Dulcie Jordan.......................Driver's Wife
Jim Michael..................................Reporter
Charlie Picerni..........................Bartender
Edwin Rochelle..............................Waiter
Joe Pine.......................................Observer
Al Beaudine, Len Felber...........Detectives
Paul Baxley, Dick Warlock.......Policemen

127

Michele

When a rash of serial murders suddenly begins in the Milwaukee area, Kolchak establishes a similarity between the new killings and the murders committed by Jack The Ripper.

It's after the first Chicago murder–a massage parlor employee carrying home a giant stuffed panda-that we join Carl and Tony at their new place of employment. After being ejected from Las Vegas and Seattle, they now work for I.N.S., the Independent News Service.

Darren McGavin, Simon Oakland

Ken Lynch, Darren McGavin

Ken Lynch, Darren McGavin

128

The killer reveals himself to possess superhuman characteristics; the police corner him but he fights them all off. Kolchak is on hand to take pictures.

Carl has been given the unenviable task by editor Tony Vincenzo of taking over the Miss Emily advice column. His colleague Updyke has been assigned the murder story, but he's not up to things, so Kolchak takes over.

Darren McGavin at his desk

Ruth McDevitt, Darren McGavin

Kolchak takes a picture

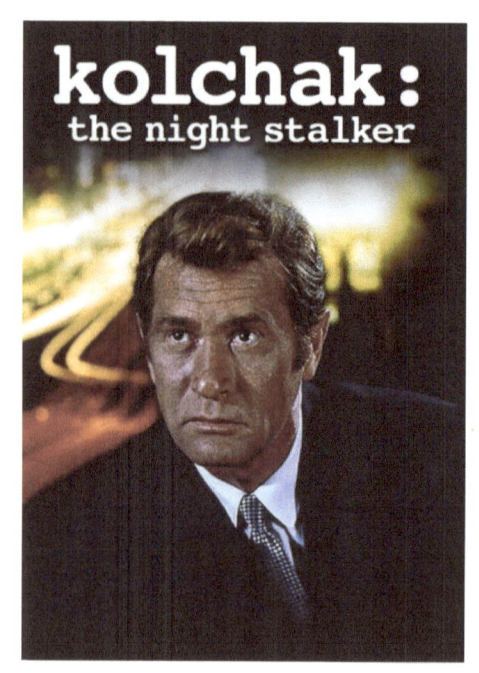

Television Poster

Kolchak searches for a letter

Jack Grinnage as Ron Updyke

Darren McGavin, Simon Oakland

Ken Lynch at the news conference

Police Captain Warren is soon at odds with Kolchak at a news conference. It seems that newswoman Jane Plumm has received a letter from The Ripper; Carl decides to find out all he can from her.

Kolchak also is aware the Ripper has superhuman strength; he jumps off a four storey building, gets hit by a car, and is shot numerous times by the police. Nothing seems to hurt him.

Kolchak's theories about this man being the original Jack the Ripper don't go over too well with boss Tony Vincenzo, or Captain Warren.

He remembers an old lady's letter to Miss Emily, mentioning an odd character living nearby.

Vincenzo gets Kolchak out of more trouble

Ken Lynch as Captain Warren

Darren McGavin typing the story

So Carl pays the woman a visit, and discovers his quarry in an old abandoned house. There, he is attacked by the Ripper, but manages to electrocute him. The house burns down; all the evidence has disappeared. Kolchak writes no story.

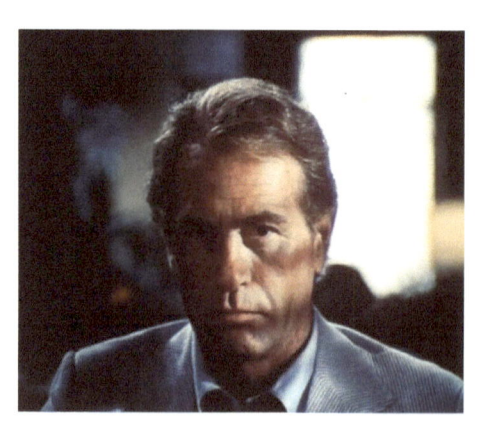

Darren McGavin as Carl Kolchak

Simon Oakland as Tony Vincenzo

Simon Oakland looking upset. What's new?

Kolchak makes his point

Simon Oakland, Jack Grinnage

Kolchak looks through the telescope

JACK THE RIPPER (1976)

DIRECTED BY JESS FRANCO

CAST

Klaus Kinski	Dr. Dennis Orloff
Josephine Chaplin	Cynthia
Herbert Fux	Charlie the Fisherman
Lina Romay	Marika Stevenson
Nikola Weisse	Frieda
Ursula V. Wiese	Miss Higgins
Hans Gaugler	John Bridger the Blind
Francine Custer	Sally Brown
Olga Gebhard	Mrs. Baxter
Angelika Arndts	Mrs. Stevenson Brown
Peter Nusch	Sergeant Ruppert
Esther Studer	Jeanny
Lorli Bucher	Miss Lulu
Mike Lederer	Coach Driver
Otto Dornbierer	Charlie's Fishing Friend
Andreas Mannkopff	Inspector Selby
Walter Baumgartner	Pianist
Regine Elsener	Blonde Girl
Angela Ritschard	Black Haired Girl
Peter Holliger	Barman
Rolf Kunz	Innkeeper
Markus Gehrig, Roman Huber	Policemen

133

Walter Baumgartner   Regine Elsener   Angela Ritschard

92 minutes

A serial killer whose mother was a prostitute starts killing streetwalkers as a way of paying back his mother for her abuse. The murders terrorize London's Whitechapel district in 1888.

Dr. Dennis Orloff resides in a boarding house in the East End of London. A respected physician by day, Orloff goes out of control and night, murdering prostitutes.

Inspector takes aim

Klaus Kinski, Josephine Chaplin

Klaus Kinski as Jack the Ripper

134

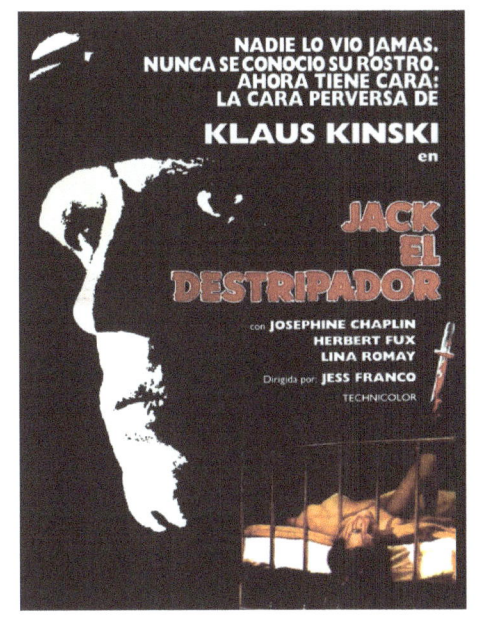

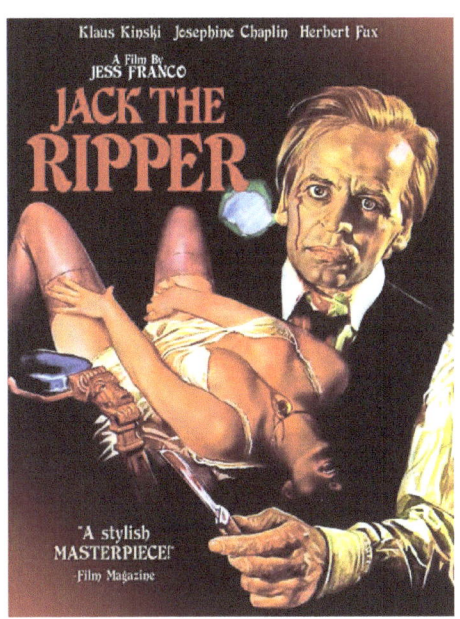

Foreign Film Poster

Film Poster

Regine Elsener, Angela Ritschard, Lorli Bucher

He searches for his prey in the London streets, as prostitutes abound at night, and eventually at a brothel until the local Inspector's girlfriend goes undercover to help catch him.

Jack the Ripper looks like something approaching a Hammer-level production, complete with period settings and lavish costumes representing Victorian England.

The results are more colorful, and have a greater visual style than director Franco's typical work, due in no small part to the highly polished cinematography of Peter Baumgartner. For once, Franco even avoids using that awful fish-eye lens we see in so many of his films.

One reviewer stated "Although this movie is completely historically inaccurate as far as Jack the Ripper goes, it's surprisingly well made for a Franco movie. Still, this is one of the few Franco films that has a more or less coherent plot to go with the occasionally impressive visuals."

Jack with another victim

Victim walking along

The film creates a tense and disturbing atmosphere, punctuated with occasionally graphic scenes of bloody violence. The effect is powerful, and the film is memorable. Perhaps Franco's best work.

Another review stated "The film is a co-production between Switzerland and West Germany and other than a few framing shots of Big Ben, was filmed abroad. I thought the settings looked quite nice. I also enjoyed the fact that much of the facts were changed; like Jack dumping body parts in the Thames."

One other reviewer said "This is a moving and horrific story about astonishing oddly murders in Whitechapel whose elusive killer results to be the famous Jack the Ripper. Grim and scary film with chills, thrills, sleaziness, ugly scenes, nudism, and lots of blood and gore.

Walter Baumgartner at the piano

Film Poster

Herbert Fux fishing

Hans Gaugler, Andreas Mannkopff

Klaus Kinski gives a creepy, remarkable portrayal of perverted sexuality and a psychologically unstable man. Along with Kinski here appear some familiar faces as Josephine Chaplin, Charlie Chaplin's daughter, Herbert Fux, and of course, Lina Romay.

This is one of the rare movies in which everything pulls together to create a weirdly compulsive atmosphere with plenty of fog, darkness, lights and shades, well shown on the photography. It is not for the squeamish."

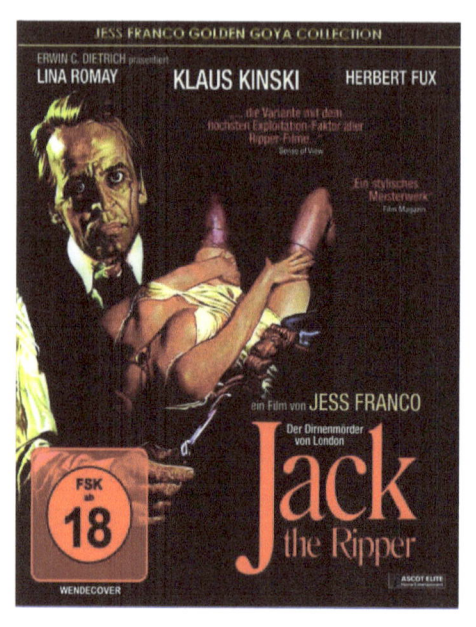

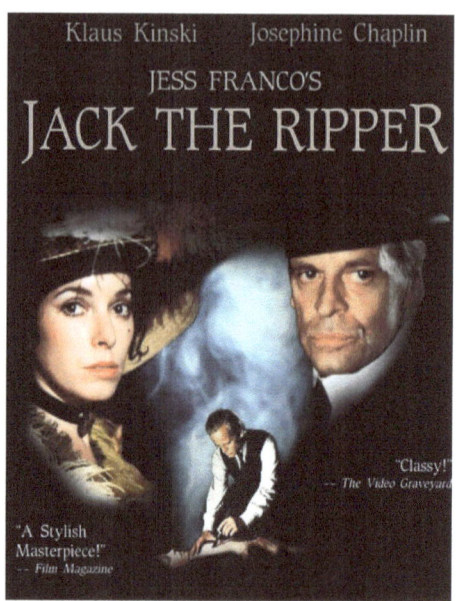

Film Poster

Film Poster

Hans Gaugler, Francine Custer

MURDER BY DECREE-1979

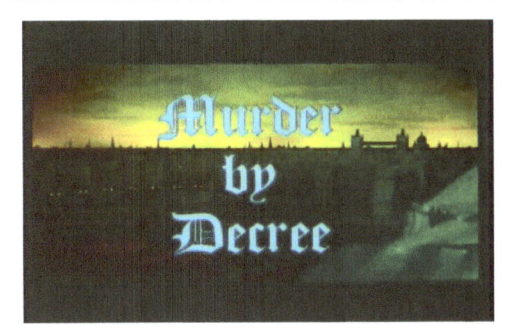

DIRECTED BY BOB CLARK

CAST

Christopher Plummer.....Sherlock Holmes
James Mason..........................Dr. Watson
Sir John Gielgud................Lord Salisbury
David Hemmings...Inspector Foxborough
Sir Anthony Quayle....Sir Charles Warren
Donald Sutherland.................Robert Lees
Frank Finlay.................Inspector Lestrade
Susan Clark............................Mary Kelly
Genevieve Bujold.................Annie Crook
Roy Lansford..............Sir Thomas Spivey
Peter Jonfield.......................William Slade
Ron Pember.................................Makins
Geoffrey Russell.............Henry Matthews
Chris Wiggins......................Doctor Hardy
Teddi Moore..............................Mrs. Lees
Victor Langley...................Prince of Wales
Pamela Abbott.............Princess Alexandra
June Brown.......................Annie Chapman
Hilary Sesta................Catherine Eddowes
Iris Fry.............................Elizabeth Stride
Robin Marchall.............Duke of Clarence
Ann Mitchell...Jane
Katherine Stark....................................Molly
Elaine Ives-Cameron.........................Ellen
Stella Courtney...................................Betty
Judy Wilson......................................Emily
Roy Pattison.................................Carroll

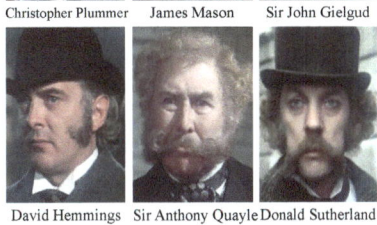

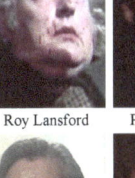

Catherine Kessler	Carrie
Ken Jones	Dock Guard
Terry Duggan	Danny
Anthony May	Lanier
Betty Woolfe	Mrs. Dobson
Peggy Ann Clifford	Lees Housekeeper
Norman Gay	Distinguished Gentleman
Richard Pescud	Doctor
Pat Brackenbury	Nurse
Michael Cashman	Constable Watkins
Dan Long	Constable Long
Jim McManus	Constable
Peter Dean, Charlie Price	P.C.s
John Tatum, Juba Kennerley, Pat Ryan, Pearl Walters, John More	Theatre Patrons

AND: Charlie Appleby, Terry Appleby, Jerry Baker, Paul Barton, Francis Batsoni, Alan Bennett, Donald Bisset, Tommy Boyle, Dave Brandon, Cassandra Chapman, Mair Coleman, Max Craig, Renee Cunliffe, Jack Dearlove, Peter Dukes, Mo Dunster, Grey Eckel, Noel Flanagan, Vic Gallucci, Jill Goldston, Ridgewell Hawkes, Carly Hawkins, Norman Hayward, Kit Hillier, Barry Holland, Ken Hutchins, John Ketteringham, Ray Knight, George Leech, Aileen Lewis, Alex Lewis, James Linton, Ned Lynch, Kai Martine, Dallas Messias, Eddie Milburn, Derek Moss, John Moyce, Stuart Myers, Maureen Nelson, Tony O'Leary, Julie Peel, Kaye Power-McGowan, Bob Ramsey, Evan Ross, Peter Roy, Eddy May Scandrett, Robin Scott, Ian Selby, Larry Sheppard, Robert Smythe, Christine Spooner, Douglas Stark, Edwin Stone, Sue Tarry, Jimmy Tippett, Cy Town, Marolyn Turk, Alan Uttley-Moore, Leslie Weekes, June West

Charlie Price | John Tatum | Juba Kennerley | Pat Ryan | Pearl Walters | John More | Donald Bisset

Max Craig | Jack Dearlove | Kit Hillier | George Leech | Aileen Lewis | Alex Lewis | Tony O'Leary

Bob Ramsey | Peter Roy | Constable | Inmate | Man 1 | Man 2 | Man 3

Victim

124 minutes

London 1888: Holmes and Watson are attending a performance at the London Opera House. When the Prince of Wales arrives, he is greeted with a chorus of boos.

Watson finds this disgraceful, and begins shouting "God save his Royal Highness." This ultimately turns the crowd's jeering into applause. "Well done old fellow-you saved the day," says Holmes.

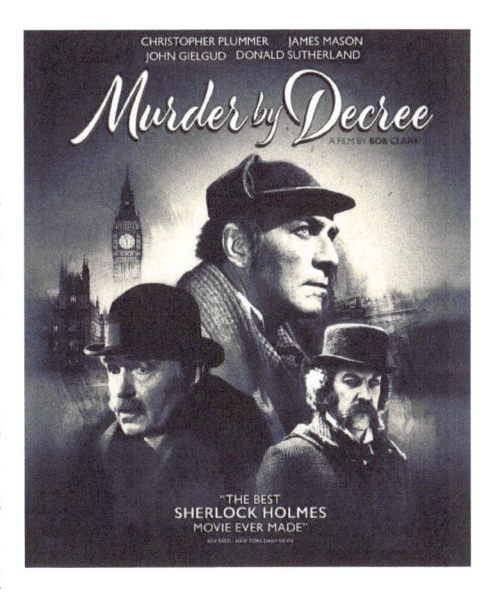

Film Poster

141

Meanwhile in the Whitechapel district of London, a woman on the street is brutally murdered. News reaches the Opera House just as the performance is over. This is not the first such killing, and Watson wonders why the authorities have not chosen to ask for the help of Sherlock Holmes.

Returning to Baker Street, Holmes is visited by three representatives of the Citizen's Committee (Whitechapel Vigilance Committee). Mr. Makins does most of the talking; they are there to enlist the help of Holmes on the recent murders.

Holmes with his signature pipe

Film Poster

Sir John Gielgud, Christopher Plummer, Geoffrey Russell

He seems strangely disinterested-almost rude-and tells them he will think it over. During the small hours of the morning, Holmes rouses Watson from sleep-there has been yet another murder.

Inspector Lestrade and his colleague Foxborough are on the scene. Sir Charles Warren, Commissioner of Scotland Yard, soon arrives, and tells Holmes to get out. In Ghoulston Street, a message is found chalked on a wall. It reads "The Juwes are not the men that will be blamed for nothing."

Film Poster

Christopher Plummer, James Mason

James Mason, Christopher Plummer

Christopher Plummer, Anthony May, Ron Pember, James Mason, Roy Pattison

Catherine Kessler, James Mason

Inspector Lestrade wants to cover it up, but Sir Charles rubs it out instead. Holmes returns with some chemicals and is able to see the message. He also realizes that he has been followed ever since he took up the case.

Down near the river, Makins is run through with a sword and left in the Thames. Holmes next seeks the help of Robert Lees, a medium who has had dreams about Jack the Ripper. When Lees went to the police he was dismissed as "a raving lunatic."

Inspector Foxborough arrives at the Lees house and tells Holmes that Sir Charles wants to see him immediately. After examining Makins' body at the morgue, Holmes meets Sir Charles, who accuses him of treason and tells him to stay out of the affair.

Next in Sir Charles' office, Holmes greets the Commissioner with a secret Masonic handshake, and tells him he knows why the chalked message was rubbed out.

Back in Baker Street, Holmes explains to Watson some of the rites and rituals of Freemasonry, and how they might apply in the Jack the Ripper murders.

Disguised as a chimney sweep, Holmes gains access to the Lees house, which is now under a police guard. Lees tells him that he actually saw the Ripper, and trailed him to his home for the police. Since the house was owned by a Royal Court physician, the police don't believe Lees.

Teddi Moore, Donald Sutherland

Genevieve Bujold, Christopher Plummer

James Mason, Chris Wiggins, Guard, Roy Pattison, Ron Pember

Going to Whitechapel alone, Watson interviews prostitues at a local pub in the guise of a reporter. He discovers that a girl called Mary Kelly may have some valuable information, but he can't find her. When one of the girls tries to rob him with the aid of a man, Watson blows a police whistle.

When the police arrive, the others tell them that Watson is the Ripper, and he is taken off to the police station. After Holmes rescues Watson from his incarceration, he attends the funeral of the latest victim, where he finds Mary Kelly in attendance.

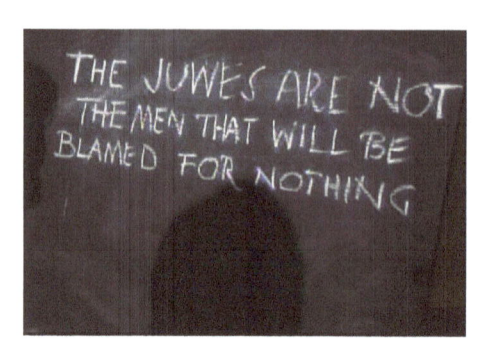

Chalked writing on the wall

James Mason, Christopher Plummer

Christopher Plummer, Susan Clark

146

Mary gives him some vital information about a woman called Annie Crook, just before both of them are run down by a cab. Holmes is left in the street with a concussion while Mary is taken away in the cab.

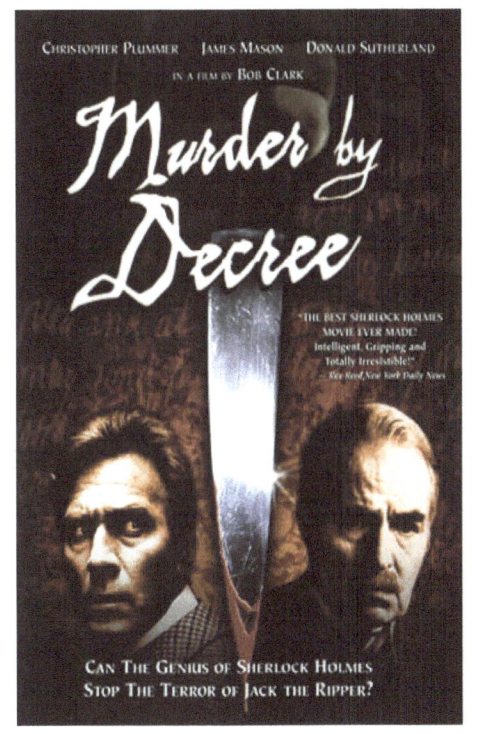

Holmes tracks Annie Crook to an asylum in Reading; she was committed by Sir Thomas Spivey, the same Royal Court physician who owned the house where Lees led the police. Although she allegedly hasn't spoken since she has been there, Holmes gets her to tell him many things when he is left alone with her.

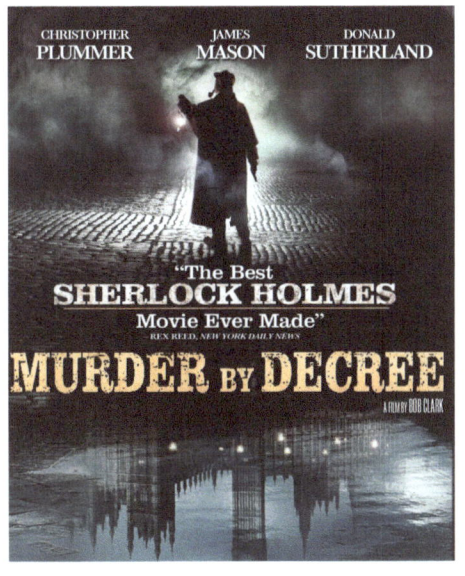

Film Poster

Film Poster

Christopher Plummer, Sir John Gielgud

147

She appears to talk in riddles, but Holmes knows exactly what she means. Annie is mostly concerned that "they" will not harm her baby, who is safe for the time being. Holmes and Watson return to the East End to resume the search for Mary Kelly.

Annie told Holmes that she entrusted her baby to Mary, and the detective thinks this is of vital importance. Realizing they are being followed, Holmes discovers his shadow is none other than Inspector Foxborough-who Holmes correctly has deduced is the head of the Radical Movement.

Sir Anthony Quayle, James Mason, Christopher Plummer

James Mason, Frank Finlay, Christopher Plummer

Christopher Plummer, James Mason

David Hemmings, Donald Sutherland

Victor Langley, Robin Marchal, Pamela Abbott

In a room in Miller's Court, Holmes and Watson discover two men who have just completed butchering Mary Kelly. One of the men stabs Watson in the shoulder with a red-hot fireplace poker, while the other, William Slade (the man wielding the sword) runs off. Foxborough, who also gives chase, is run through by Slade's sword; Holmes eventually corners him near the docks. A terrific fight ensues, with Slade eventually being hanged to death in some netting.

Some time later, Holmes has a secret meeting with Prime Minister Lord Salisbury, Home Secretary Henry Matthews, and Sir Charles Warren, where he explains the identity of Jack the Ripper, and the motives behind the Whitechapel murders.

James Mason, Christopher Plummer

Roy Lansford, Christopher Plummer

TIME AFTER TIME (1979)

DIRECTED BY NICHOLAS MEYER

CAST

Malcolm McDowell	H.G. Wells
David Warner	John Stevenson
Mary Steenburgen	Amy Robbins
Charles Cioffi	Lieutenant Mitchell
Kent Williams	Assistant
Andonia Katsaros	Mrs. Turner
Patti D'Arbanville	Shirley
James Garrett	Edwards
Keith McConnell	Harding
Leo Lewis	Richardson
Byron Webster	McKay
Laurie Main	Inspector Gregson
Karin Mary Shea	Jenny
Geraldine Baron	Carol
Joseph Maher	Adams
Michael Evans	Sergeant
Ray Reinhardt	Jeweler
Bob Shaw	Bank Officer
Stu Klitsner	Clergyman
Judith Burnett	Ann
Shirley Marchant	Dolores
Bill Bradley	Pawnbroker
Mike Gainey	London Bobby
Read Morgan	Booking Cop
Larry J. Blake	Guard
Clement St. George	Bobby
Gene Hartline	Cab Driver

Antonie Becker, Hilda Haynes.......Nurses
John Colton, Jim Haynie, Earl Nichols, Wayne Storm............................Policemen

AND: Glenn Carlson, Rita Conde, James Cranna, Lou Felder, Corey Feldman, Anthony Garibaldi, Anthony Gordon, Shelley Hack, Gail Hyatt, Dan Leegan, Doug Morrisson, Liz Roberson, Nicholas Shields, Regina Waldron

Bob Shaw Stu Klitsner Shirley Marchant
Bill Bradley Larry J. Blake Gene Hartline
Antonie Becker Hilda Haynes Rita Conde
Corey Feldman Shelley Hack Nicholas Shields

112 minutes

At a dinner party in the home of H.G. Wells in Victorian London, the writer shows his guests a time machine that he has built, explaining to them how it works. Shortly afterwards, police arrive looking for Jack the Ripper-whom they believe was one of the guests-John Stevenson. When Wells goes to his laboratory, the time machine is gone. So is Stevenson. Since Stevenson doesn't have all the keys to the machine, it returns to Wells' laboratory. Wells can see that Stevenson has escaped 90 years into the future, so he takes off after him.

It is now 1979. Wells' time machine is in a San Francisco museum. Wells is not too pleased with the future, which is full of noise and chaos, not to mention wars, crimes, and all sorts of other problems.

Figuring that Stevenson would need to exchange English pounds for dollars, as we are now in the United States, Wells goes to several banks and learns from Amy Robbins, an employee of the Chartered Bank of London, that Stevenson was in fact there. Amy recommended the Hyatt Hotel to Stevenson.

Malcolm McDowell as H.G. Wells

David Warner as John Stevenson

Byron Webster, right

153

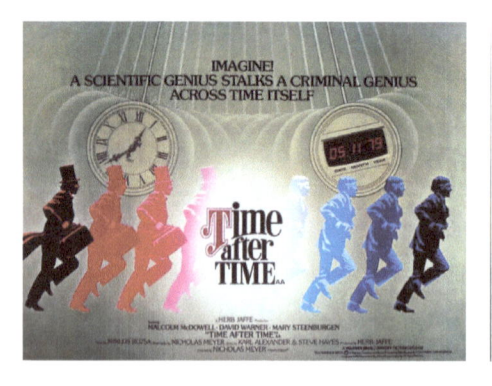

Film Poster   Film Poster

Malcolm McDowell, Mary Steenburgen

Wells goes to the hotel and finds him. Stevenson actually likes the crime and violence of the future. He tells Wells: "Ninety years ago, I was a freak. Now... I'm an amateur." Wells demands he return to the past to face justice, but Stevenson instead attempts to steal the time machine's return key from him. This doesn't work; Stevenson takes off with Wells chasing after him; Stevenson is hit by a car and taken to a hospital. At the hospital emergency room, Wells asks for a tall Englishman who was struck by a motor car. Mistakenly, he gets the impression that Stevenson has died from his injuries.

154

Wells meets up with Amy Robbins again and she initiates a romance. Meanwhile a released Stevenson returns to the bank to exchange more money; suspecting that it was Amy who had led Wells to him, he finds out where she lives.

Wells, hoping to convince her of the truth, takes a highly skeptical Amy three days into the future. Once there, she is aghast to see a newspaper headline revealing her own murder.

Mary Steenburgen, Malcolm McDowell

David Warner, Mary Steenburgen

David Warner, Malcolm McDowell

Wells tries to convince Amy they must go back-to prevent the other girl's murder as well as her own. When they phone the police, Stevenson kills once more; since Wells seems to know quite a lot he is arrested and held by the police.

Wells under arrest

Foreign Film Poster

Malcom McDowell shows his friends the key

Malcolm McDowell & David Warner

Malcolm McDowell, Mary Steenburgen

Malcolm McDowell, David Warner

Malcolm McDowell as H.G. Wells

Mary Steenburgen, Malcolm McDowell

Wells finally persuades the police that Amy is in real trouble. They all go to her apartment, where they find the dismembered remains of a woman–they all think it's Amy. Wrong! It's a co-worker; Amy is now in the clutches of Stevenson, who wants the key to the time machine.

Wells agrees to his terms; at the museum, Wells gives Stevenson the key, and Amy escapes. As Stevenson starts up the time machine, Herbert removes the vaporizing equalizer from it.

As Herbert had explained earlier, this causes the machine to remain in place while its passenger is sent travelling endlessly through time. Wells now realizes he must return to his own time, and when there, destroy the machine. Amy decides to go with him.

The Time Machine

David Warner, Malcolm McDowell

Wells watches the time machine taking off

JACK THE RIPPER (1988)

DIRECTED BY DAVID WICKES

CAST

Michael Caine..Inspector Frederick Abberline
Ray McAnally.................Sir William Gull
Lewis Collins.....Sergeant George Godley
Jane Seymour....................Emma Prentiss
Armand Assante..........Richard Mansfield
Ken Bones..................Robert James Lees
Susan George.............Catherine Eddowes
Jon Laurimore....Inspector John Spratling
Harry Andrews..................Wynne Baxter
Hugh Fraser................Sir Charles Warren
Lysette Anthony..............Mary Jane Kelly
Michael Gothard...................George Lusk
Edward Judd................Chief Supt. Arnold
Roger Ashton-Griffiths................Rodman
Peter Armitage.................Sergeant Kerby
Michael Hughes..........Dr. Rees Llewellyn
T.P. McKenna...........................O'Connor
Richard Morant........Dr. Theodore Acland
George Sweeney.....................John Netley
Gerald Sim....Dr. George Bagster Phillips
Ronald Hines..................Henry Matthews
Denys Hawthorne.....Sir Robert Anderson
Jonathan Moore................Benjamin Bates
David Swift........................Lord Salisbury
Gary Love..Derek
Ann Castle................................Lady Gull
Angela Crow....................Elizabeth Stride

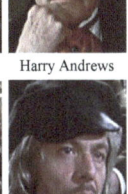

Deirdre Costello...............Annie Chapman
Kelly Cryer....................................Annette
Gertan Klauber.............Louis Diemschutz
Jon Croft..................................Thackeray
Peter Hughes................................Paulson
John Normington...........................Dresser
Eric Mason....................................Publican
George Malpas............................Old Man
Desmond Askew.........................Copy Boy
Trevor Baxter..................................Lanyon
Mike Carnell...........................Newsvendor
Marc Culwick............Prince Albert Victor
John Dair.................................Isenschmid
Roy Evans...............................Doorkeeper
John Fletcher...........................PC Watkins
Sheridan Forbes................................Millie
Martin Friend.........................Newsvendor
Christopher Fulford............Sergeant Brent
David Ryall......................Thomas Bowyer
Gary Shail................................Billy White
Bruce Green...............................John Pizer
Ronald Nunnery...............................Davis
Sandra Payne.........................Mrs. Acland
Neville Phillips..............Cabinet Secretary
Norman Warwick......................Richardson
Brian Weske......................................Porter
Iain Rattray...............................Tough Cop
Frank Jarvis...................................Passerby
Bernadette Milnes......Woman in Doorway
Mike Lewin............................Duty Guard
Rod Lewis...................................Mortician
Rikki Harnet.............................Pickpocket

AND: David Adams, Joy Adams, Leslie Adams, Hazel Allen, Peter Allen, Tony Allen, Andrew Andreas, Maraquita Annis, Charlie Appleby, Alicia Armstrong, Jack Armstrong, Jack Arrow, Richard Atherton, Douglas Auchterlonie, Peter Avella, Jackie

Avey, Sheila Aza, Norman Bacon, John Bailey, Redmond Bailey, Frances Baker, Jerry Baker, Jon Baker, George Ballantine, Bernard Barnsley, Ann Barrass, Andy Barrett, Sean Barry, Francis Batsoni, Roy Beck, Hyma Beckley, Alan Bennett, Paul Beradi, Kid Berg, Barbara Bermel, Ronnie Berry, Harry Bilgorri, David Billa, Brian Bowes, Peter Brayham, James Brett, Mike Brown, Woolf Byrne, Rodney Cardiff, Ted Carroll, Jack Carter, Tony Castleton, Cassandra Chapman, Dave Church, Ina Clare, Mickey Clarke, Norton Clarke, Norman Cleary, John Clifford, Maurice Connor, Ken Coombs, Douglas Cooper, George Lane Cooper, Harold Coyne, Robert Crake, Alan Crisp, Bert Crome, Renee Cunliffe, Claire Davenport, Lionel DeClerk, Gary Dean, Jack Dearlove, Warwick Denny, Peter Diamond, John Dodd, John Doye, Grey Eckel, John Emms, Shirley English, Peter Evans, Joyce Everson, Roy Everson, Bradley Farmer, David Field, Harry Fielder, Vincent Fleming, Dorothy Ford, Eden Fox, Terry Francis, Otto Friese, Jack Frost, Iris Fry, Salo Gardner, Norman Gay, Alan Gibbs, Anthony Gilding, Charles Gilliard, Pat Gorman, Tommy Graham, Isaac Grand, Charlie Gray, Richard Gregory, Ron Gregory, Fred Griffiths, June Hammond, Peter Hannon, Aidan Harrington, Alan Harris, Tina Hart, Eileen Harvey, Carly Hawkins, Noel Hawkins, Rosemary Hazeldine, Renee Heimer, Walter Henry, Kit Hillier, Walter Henry, Mark Henson, George Hilsdon, George Holdcroft, Bob Holmes, Lew Hooper, Terence Horan, Tom Humphries, Clive Hurst, Ken Hutchins, Brian Jackson, Jazzer Jeyes, Malcolm Johns, Fred Johnson, Martin Kennedy, Michael Kennedy, Juba Kennerley, Cyril Kent, John Ketteringham, Richard King, Paul Kirby, Barbara Lampshire, David Lane, Anthony Lang, Roy Lansford, Tommy Little, Martin Lyder, Ned Lynch, Marjorie Lyons, James Linton, Jay McGrath, Alison McGuire, Colin McKenzie, Don McLean, Wyn McLeod, Christina Mackey, Jack Mandeville, Alf Mangan, Ben Mansworth, Louis Matto, Mary Maxfield, Alan Meachum, Tony Mendleson, Dallas Messias, Manny Michael, Jack Midwinter, Colin Mills, Monty Morriss, James Muir, Mike Mungarvan, Dave Murphy, Maureen Nelson, Kay Noone, Alec North, Rowland Ogden, Tony O'Leary, George Oliver, Gerald Paris, Sammy Pasha, James Payne, Sandra Payne, Julie Peel, Patsy Peters, Paul Phillips, Dido Plumb, Terry Plummer, Greg Powell, Kaye Power-McGowan, Charlie Price, Paul Puig, Bob Ramsey, Mike Randall, Edith Raye, Charles Rayford, Fred Reford, Mike Reynell, Steve Ricard, Henry Roberts, Bessie Rogers, John Rogers, Laurie Rose, Peter Roy, Wendy Rudin, Pat Ryan, Terry Sach, Ivan Santon, Terry Sartain, Ray Schock, Jimmy Scott, Bunny Seaman, Ken Sedd, Roy Seeley, Ian Selby, Richard Sheekey, Sandy Shelton, Larry Sheppard, Jack Silk. Jeffrey Silk, Tina Simmons, Danny Sinclair, Sadie Slade, Tony Smart, Esme Smythe, Robert Smythe, Anthony Snell, Byron Sotiris, Anita St. John, Guy Standeven, Douglas Stark, Alan Starkey, Mike Stevens, Fred Stroud, Barry Summerford, Sue Tarry, John Tatum, Zelda Tatum, Mark Taylor, Colin Thom

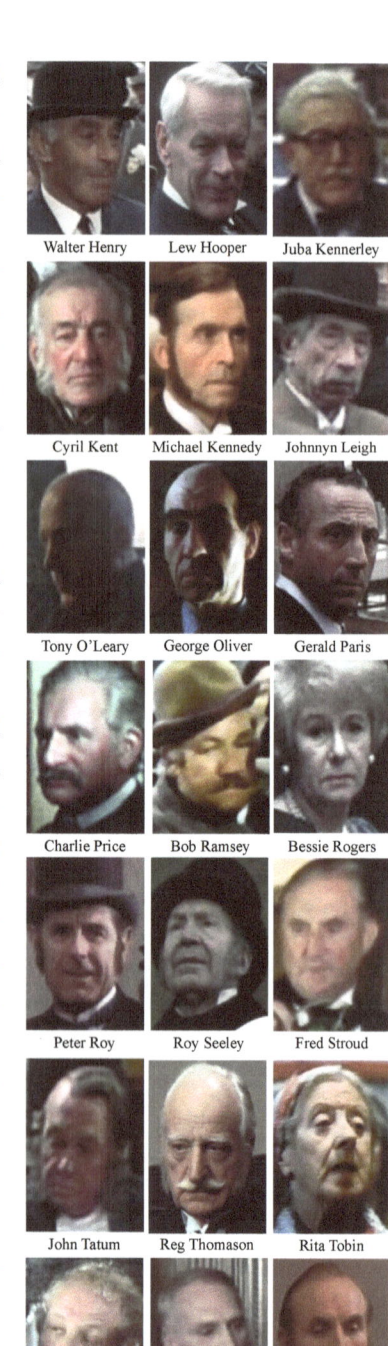

Reg Thomason, Bill Tickner, Harry Tierney, Rita Tobin, John Triplett, Marolyn Turk, Reg Turner, Alan Uttley-Moore, Harry Van Engel, Annette Vellender, Sheila Vivian, Ron Watkins, Jeff Wayne, Chris Webb, Trevor Wedlock, Leslie Weekes, Tommy Weldin, June West, Paul Weston, Tommy Winward, Fred Woods, Syd Wragg, Bob Wright, Margaret Yard

Fred Woods    Man 1    Man 2

Man 3

188 minutes

August, 1888: Mary Ann Nichols is slaughtered in the streets of London beginning the reign of terror of the murderer commonly known as Jack The Ripper. More victims start to appear scattered around Whitechapel, all as savagely butchered as the next. With the threat of a popular or even Anarchist uprising and the government as unpopular as ever, the police and the ruling class are desperate to see an end to the killing spree.

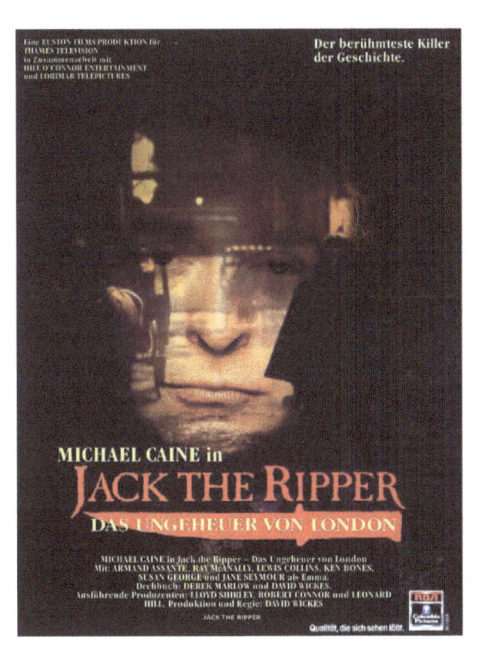

German Film Poster

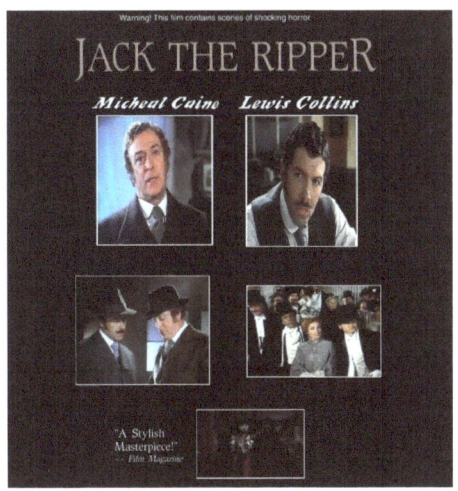

Film Poster

163

Alcoholic police detective Inspector Frederick Aberline is put in charge of the investigation despite his alcoholism or maybe because of it, since if all else fails, he'll make a fantastic scapegoat.

Together with Sergeant George Godley, Abberline is finding suspects everywhere. One of them could be the flamboyant actor Richard Mansfield who is currently playing Jekyll and Hyde on the stage in a performance so diabolically convincing that Abberline can't help wondering where Mansfield finds the inspiration.

Gary Shail, Jonathan Moore, Armand Assante, Michael Caine, Lewis Collins, Ken Bones, Edward Judd, Michael Gothard

Lewis Collins, Michael Caine

George Sweeney, Lewis Collins

Richard Morant, Ray McAnally

Peter Hughes, Jonathan Moore

Michaeil Caine, Michael Hughes

The famous spiritualist Robert James Lees is consulted, with intriguing results that bring Abberline and Godley closer to the truth. As the killer prepares for his worst crime yet, the Metropolitan Police are pressuring Abberline to find him before Whitechapel is set ablaze by rioters who fear for their women's lives. They see an opportunity to force the city into creating better living conditions in the East End. Jack the Ripper seems to have proven to be one of the most enduring criminals of modern history.

Ken Bones, Michael Caine

Richard Morant, Michael Hughes, Marc Culwick, Lewis Collins, Michael Caine, Ray McAnally, George Sweeney, Hugh Fraser, Roger Ashton-Griffiths

Ray McAnally, Jon Laurimore, Edward Judd

As the mutilated corpses of other "shilling whores" turn up in the same area, London's tabloid journalists-particularly Benjamin Bates of The Star-whip up a public frenzy. The killer is nicknamed Jack the Ripper after a letter bearing that soubriquet and supposedly from the killer, is forwarded to Scotland Yard.

As the Ripper terrorizes London, public outrage erupts throughout the country, and Police Commissioner Sir Charles Warren fears that a revolution is in the air in London's East End.

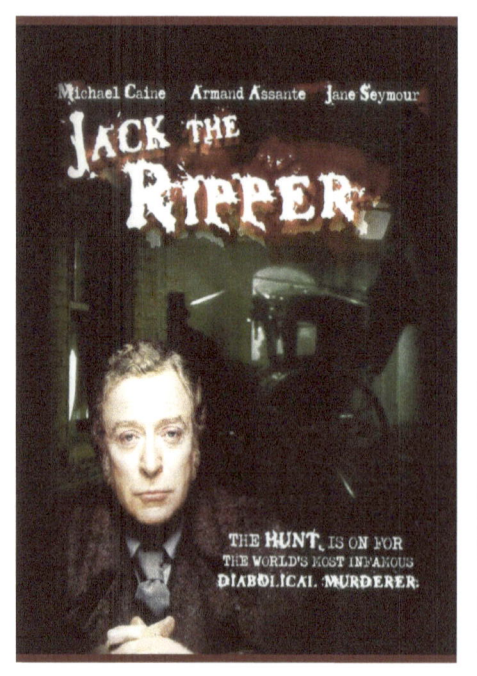

Film Poster

David Ryall, John Laurimore

Hugh Fraser, Michael Caine

Lewis Collins, Ken Bones

Jon Laurimore, Peter Armitage

The police and the authorities want the murders solved at any cost, but Abberline and Godley face huge obstacles as they search for the truth- and hindrance from their superiors when the killer is finally unmasked. This version is quite an effective piece of television drama. Though they had originally started to film on video with a different cast (with Barry Foster in the lead), a vast sum of money was put up by CBS on the condition they made it into a much bigger production with U.S. recognizable stars.

Ray McAnally, Ann Castle

Jonathan Moore, Michael Gothard

Jane Seymour, Jonathan Moore, T.P. McKenna

The production value reflects the fresh injection of money seemingly going into the sets and the period costumes; the global feel is not really that of a TV drama but rather a film.

The film was originally split into two parts to be shown on different nights. The direction is generally quite good with the cast performing well. The overall quality of the production makes it a good piece of well researched TV drama that stands up to repeated viewings and the test of time.

Jon Laurimore, Michael Caine

Lewis Collins, Michael Caine

Hugh Fraser, Michael Caine, Ray McAnally

In 1888, when the real Jack the Ripper was terrorizing London, the court records were ordered to be vaulted for one hundred years and the details of the case kept confidential.

This film claims to be based on these top secret Home Office files; the filmmakers believe their ending the correct solution to the mystery. This is an outstanding film, especially so given that it was made for television.

Edward Judd, Harry Andrews

Peter Armitage, Jon Laurimore, Gary Love

Michael Gothard, Lewis Collins, Michael Caine

The character portrayals are solid, as is the screenplay, but the acting, top notch work from everyone, takes the spotlight. Michael Caine, who plays the lead detective on the case, won a well-deserved Golden Globe award for his performance.

Eric Mason, Susan George

Site of the second murder

George Sweeney, Eric Mason

THE SECRET IDENTITY OF JACK THE RIPPER (1988)

DIRECTED BY LOUIS J. HORVITZ

CAST

Peter Ustinov	Host
Regis J. Cordic	Announcer
Dr. William Eckert	Forensic Pathologist
Jan Leeming	Reporter
Anne Mallalieu	Queen's Counsel
William Waddell	Scotland Yard Man
Dr. David Thomas	Curator of Public Records
Paul Begg, Frank Spiering	Research Experts
Martin Fido, Donald Rumbelow	Crime Historians
John Douglas, Roy Hazelwood	F.B.I. Special Agents
Daniel Farson, Melvin Harris, Colin Wilson	Authors

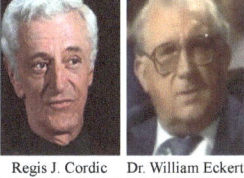

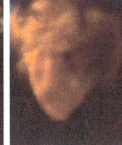

Aaron Kosminski   Montague John Druitt   Prince Albert Victor   Sir William Gull   Alice Crook   Chief Inspector Donald Swanson   Queen Victoria

Sir Robert Anderson   Walter Sickert   Robert Stephenson

80 minutes

A panel of experts examines the five main suspects in the Jack the Ripper murders and determines which of them is the most likely to have committed the crimes.

This is a documentary of the famous unsolved case of 1888 in the Whitechapel district of London. After a brief summary of the case, the program structure alternates between three major elements.

Film Poster

Peter Ustinov with small booklet

More East End residents, 1888

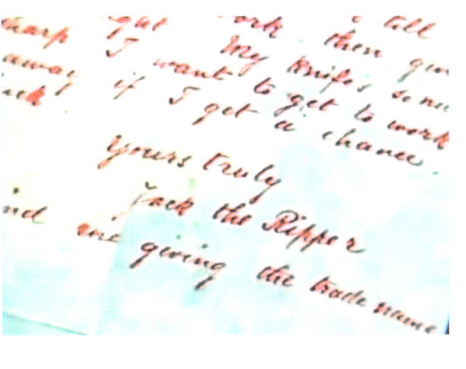

Jack the Ripper letter

George Hutchinson smoking a pipe

East End people, 1888

Police outside Mary Kelly's room

Message on the wall in Goulston Street

The first element is a re-creation of the murders of the five canonical victims: Nichols, Chapman, Stride, Eddowes, and Kelly. A second element is an analysis of the crimes by five crime "experts."

And a third element consists of a basic profile of the five leading ripper suspects. Added to these three program elements are discussions from authors and researchers, who give their opinions.

173

Peter Ustinov hosts the program and directs the flow of discussion among the three major elements. The re-creations are quite good. Costumes, production design, acting, and dim lighting convey what must be a fairly realistic Whitechapel setting at the time of the murders. Background music is appropriately eerie and mysterious.

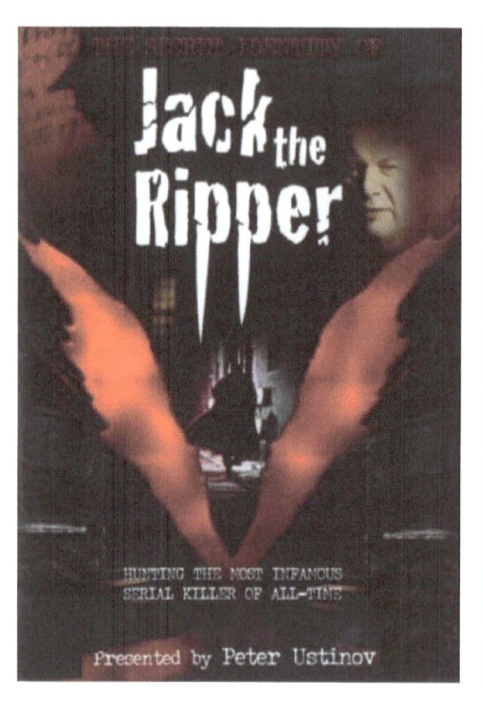

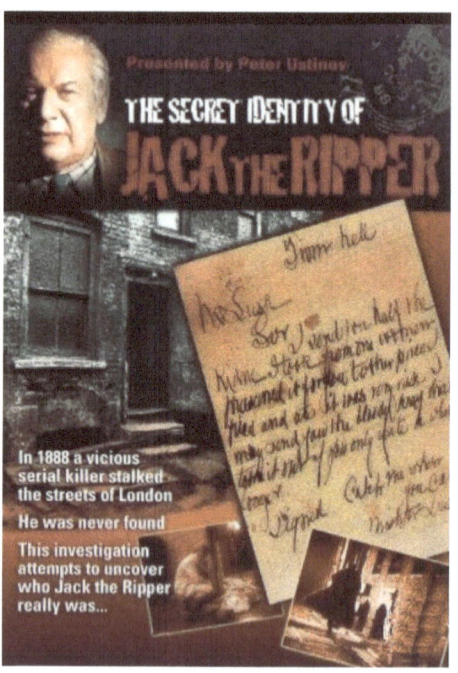

Film Poster

Film Poster

Film Poster

The five "experts" sit at a semi-round table with a live audience behind them. The experts are from both the U.S. and England, and all are affiliated with some powerful institution.

The five leading suspects have their photos on a wall behind Ustinov. Given that there have been dozens if not hundreds of suspects proposed as the Ripper, the program gives no indication of how the top five were selected.

Dr. William Eckert, Peter Ustinov

Donald Swanson, Sir Robert Anderson

Five suspects on the board

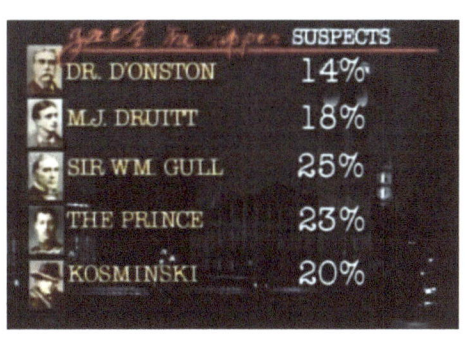

Chart of poll taken as to who was Jack the Ripper

Peter Ustinov with the portraits

Essex Wharf building

At the end, each of the five experts gives his or her opinion on which of the five suspects is most likely Jack the Ripper. Since the "experts" represent official institutions, their choice is institutionally safe and predictable. The program goes out of its way to avoid sensationalism and contrivance.

All five unanimously believe that Aaron Kosminski was Jack the Ripper; they all state their reasons and are in agreement. It was noted that after Kosminski was sent to an asylum, the killings stopped.

Whitechapek residents

Peter Ustinov as the host

P.C. John Neil discovers the body of Polly Nichols

THE RIPPER (1997)

DIRECTED BY JANET MEYERS

CAST

Patrick Bergen........Inspector Jim Hansen
Gabrielle Anwar....................Florry Lewis
Samuel West..........................Prince Albert
Michael York..............Sir Charles Warren
Adam Couper..........Sergeant Tommy Bell
Essie Davis....................Evelyn Bookman
Olivia Hamnett..................Lady Margaret
Karen Davitt...........................Mary Kelly
Damien Pree......................Officer Peters
Stewart Morritt................................Cullen
Kevin Miles.................Sir William Fraser
John Gregg.....................Dr. William Gull
Frank Whitten...........................Dr. Pearce
Peter Collingwood.....................Chalmers
Josephine Keen................................Lizzie
Lisle Jones......................Thomas Delaney
Anthony Morton.........................Cartman
Christopher Kemp.....................Milkman
Denzil Howson..........................Doorman
Caroline Huff.............................Spectator
Jessica Muschamp.............................Maid
David Clisby.................................Big Man
Richie Akers..........................Small Man
John Murphy..............................Old Gent
Sally-Anne Upton......................Bartender
Curtis Barnott..........................Young Cop
Maureen Edwards...........................Matron

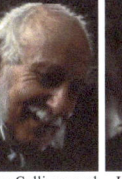

177

Suzy Cato............................Prissy Woman
Peter Stratford.....................Snobbish Man
Peter Hardy................................Patrician
Shaun Murphy...............................Tenor
Grant Smith................................Baritone
Dawn Klingberg......................Old Woman
Dean Barton-Ancliffe......................Drunk
Timothy Wood................................Valet
John Turner.................................Guard
Colin Duckworth...................Major Domo
Michael Fry...............................Captain
Monty Maizells...........................Old Man
Andrew Shortell.........Police Photographer
Stephen McIntyre..........................Pianist
Hamish Hughes, Lawrence Price...............
.....................................Audience Members
Justin Parslow, Stephen Sheehan...............
....Policemen
Di Diddle, Anny Fodor, Ross Mathers, Santha Press..................Theatrical Troupe
Cheryl Batten, Dean Crighton, Cody Harris, Fred Lewis, Terry Tulk.............Coach Drivers

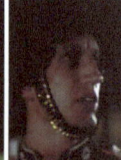

96 minutes

In 1888, in London, a prostitute is slaughtered on the street. The Scotland Yard Chief Inspector Jim Hansen is in charge of the investigation and realizes that the killer is a person with skill in dissection.

Hansen belongs to the lower class and aspires to socially climb. Soon there are other murders and the ex-prostitute Florry Lewis witnesses the killer killing a prostitute and is forced to go to the precinct to provide a lead to Scotland Yard.

Inspector Hansen assigns Sergeant Tommy Bell to protect Florry and he investigates the murder cases. Prince Albert Victor, who is the heir of the throne of England, becomes his prime suspect but his chief Sir Charles Warren tells that they need to have strong evidence against the Prince to proceed with the case.

Film Poster

Adam Couper as Sergeant Bell

Patrick Bergin, Michael York

Samuel West, Timothy Wood

Essie Davis, Patrick Bergin

Patrick Bergin, Samuel West

Samuel West, Patrick Bergin

Gabrielle Anwar, Josephine Keen

Patrick Bergen playing cards

Sir Charles decides to use Florry as bait but Inspector Hansen has fallen in love with her and objects. But his chief makes clear that this is the only way to stop the Ripper. A trap is set, but the Prince escapes.

Hansen follows him back to the palace, where Hansen gains entry by knocking out a guard, then gets inside and subdues the Prince. The Prince soon disappeared from public life; sometime later is was announced that he died of influenza.

The focus of this film is police inspector James Hansen, the chief inspector on the Jack the Ripper case, as well as his involvement with the upper class, including Prince Albert Victor Edward.

There are also two romantic interests for Hansen; Florry Lewis, an ex-prostitute who witnesses the killer leaving a crime scene, and Evelyn Bookman, who Hansen's aristocratic friends favour.

Michael York, Olivia Hamnett

Prince and entourage at the opera

Prince just set fire to the horse

Jack the Ripper's first victim

Adam Couper, Patrick Bergin, Damien Pree

The cinematography and lighting dwell on a range of browns and grays, giving something like a sepia-toned atmosphere of looking at old photographs, but at the same time nothing about it feels artificial- it is very naturalistic.

The colors are not achieved through any kind of unusual film processing, and the locations, sets, and costumes authentically transport you to the world of late 19th century London.

Samuel West, Olivia Hamnett. Michael York

Olivia Hamnett, Essie Davis

Patrick Bergin, Gabrielle Anwar

Michael York, Patrick Bergin

Patrick Bergin, Peter Collingwood

Patrick Bergin, Essie Davis

182

FROM HELL (2001)

DIRECTED BY ALBERT HUGHES, ALLEN HUGHES

CAST

Johnny Depp....Inspector Frederick Abberline
Heather Graham.......................Mary Kelly
Ian Holm..........................Sir William Gull
Ian Richardson............Sir Charles Warren
Robbie Coltrane.....Sergeant Peter Godley
Terence Harvey.............Benjamin Kidney
Jason Flemyng........................John Netley
Paul Rhys...................................Dr. Ferral
Katrin Cartlidge...............Annie Chapman
Susan Lynch......................Elizabeth Stride
Lesley Sharp...............Catherine Eddowes
Annabelle Apsion................Polly Nichols
Estelle Skornik...................................Ada
Nicholas McGaughey.............Officer Bolt
Joanna Page...........................Annie Crook
Mark Dexter........................Albert Sickert
Danny Midwinter.........Constable Withers
Samantha Spiro.................Martha Tabram
David Schofield.........................McQueen
Peter Eyre..........................Lord Hallsham
Ian McNeice........Coroner Robert Drudge
Donald Douglas.............Hospital Director
James Greene...............Masonic Governor
John Owens...........Marylebone Governor
Bryon Fear..............................Robert Best
Cliff Parisi..........................Mac-Bartender
Sophia Myles...............Victoria Abberline

Ralph Ineson....................................Gordie
Amy Huck...............................Gull's Maid
Rupert Farley......................Doss Landlord
Liz Moscrop.......................Queen Victoria
Roger Frost..................Sidewalk Preacher
Steve Shepherd...........................Constable
Al Ashton................................Stonecutter
Poppy Rogers..........................Alice Crook
Bruce Byron........................Annie's Father
Melanie Hill......................Annie's Mother
Vincent Franklin....................George Lusk
Louise Atkins.............................Prostitute
Anthony Parker.....................John Merrick
Carey Thring........................Photographer
Vladimir Kulhavy..........Rag & Bone Man
Graham Kent.......................Records Clerk
Rupert Holliday-Evans.....................Sailor
Simon Harrison....................Thomas Bond
Paul Moody...........................Young Doctor
Gerry Grennell.................Funeral Minister
Tony Tang....................Opium Den Owner
Stephen Milton.................Medical Student
Lichelli Lazar Lea.............London Wench
Glen Berry, Charlie Parish.........Labourers
David Fisher, Andy Linden......Carpenters
Steve Chaplin, Dominic Cooper, Gary Powell...Constables

AND: Diane Ash, Raymond Ash, Alan Bennett, Dominic Cooper, Steve Dent, Alan James, Michael Laborde, Andy Linden, Loucas Louca, Dinny Powell, Kaye Power-McGowan, Edwin Stone

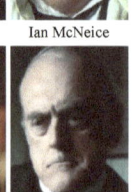

Vincent Franklin Anthony Parker Carey Thring Graham Kent Rupert Holliday-Evans Paul Moody Gerry Grennell

Tony Tang Glen Berry

122 minutes

In London in 1888 it was estimated as many as 80,000 women worked as prostitutes, many of them in the Whitechapel and Spitalfields areas.

Many could only earn the price of a few drinks, or a bed for the night. Mary Kelly was one such woman. Her friend Annie is kidnapped and drawn into a conspiracy with links high up. The kidnapping is soon followed by the gruesome murder of another woman, Martha Tabram, and it becomes apparent that they are being hunted down, one by one as the various prostitutes are murdered and mutilated.

Film Poster

Johnny Depp as Inspector Abberline

The murders of Martha and her companions grabs the attention of the police, who assign to the investigation a brilliant yet troubled man, Frederick Abberline, whose police work is often aided by his psychic visions.

Abberline's investigations reveal that the murders, while gruesome, imply that an educated person is responsible due to the precise and almost surgical method used.

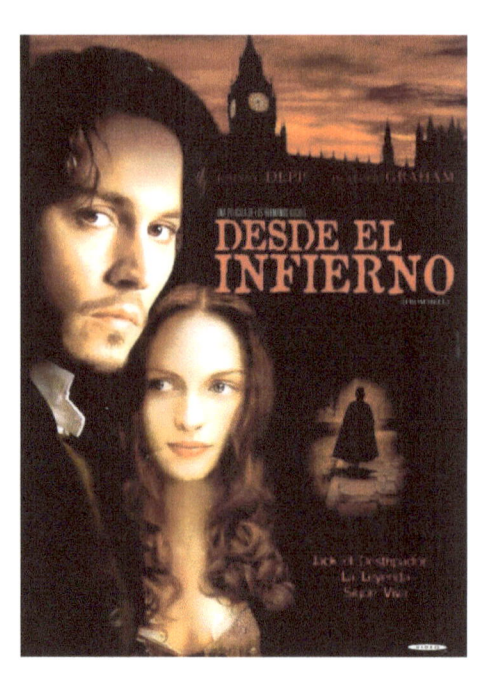

Film Poster

Foreign Film Poster

Robbie Coltrane, Johnny Depp, Ian Richardson

Annie is found a few days later in an asylum having been lobotomized after officials and doctors supposedly found her to be insane. It is implied this was done to silence her. Abberline consults Sir William Gull, a physician to the Royal Family, drawing on his experience and knowledge of medicine.

These findings coupled with his superiors impeding his investigations, point to a darker and organized conspiracy. Abberline becomes deeply involved with the case, which takes on personal meaning to him when he and Mary begin to fall in love.

Ian Holm as Sir William Gull

The Ripper takes another victim

Katrin Cartlidge, Lesley Sharp, Heather Graham

187

Abberline deduces that Masonic influence is definitely present in these crimes. His superior, a high ranking Freemason himself, then makes direct intervention and suspends Abberline. It is then revealed that Sir William Gull is the killer.

Johnny Depp, Robbie Coltrane

Heather Graham, Johnny Depp

Robbie Coltrane as Sergeant Godley

Paul Rhys and friends

Johnny Depp, Ian Holm

Discovery of another victim

188

He has been killing the witnesses to Prince Eddy's forbidden marriage to Annie, the prostitute who bore his illegitimate daughter, who is therefore the heir to the British throne.

London location scene

Katrin Cartlidge, Susan Lynch

What's this? A stalk of grapes?

Gull himself is a Freemason and his increasingly sinister behavior lends an insight into his murderous, but calculated mind. Rather than publicly charge Gull, it is decided that he be lobotomized to protect the Royal family from the scandal.

Gull defiantly states he has no equal among men, remaining without guilt right up to his lobotomy, resulting in him becoming an invalid just as Annie had been.

Robbie Coltrane, Danny Midwinter

Johnny Depp, Heather Graham

Ian Richardson as Sir Charles Warren